First Time Press Release Number: 6
Frist Time Press 2021 Catalog Release Number: 2
Orginal Release Date: 03/01/2021

Published by First Time Press
a protected series of S.C. TreeHouse, LLC
3928 Pattentown Rd. Ooltewah, USA, TN 37363
www.firsttimepress.sctreehouse.com

Printed in the United States of America

Printed in the United States of America.
ISBN: 978-1-7366172-2-9

Edited by Laura Schonlau
Designed by Christopher D. Stewart

ISBN 978-1-7366172-2-9

brutally broken
Beautifully Redeemed

by

LAURA SCHONLAU
Stories from
The highlight reel of my own life.

First Time Press
A Storytellers Company

WELCOME

First Time
Press

Welcome

Thank you for choosing to read this First Time Press book. As First Time Press we exist to give promising authors a platform to publish their early works. Since our founding, First Time Press has eagerly sought out and received submissions from authors worldwide looking for a chance to be noticed for their extraordinary creations.

What you are about to experience is raw talent. The following book has not been altered or edited by us (the publisher); instead, it is left exactly as the author wrote it. This is a showcase of an unaltered creation that we hope can inspire you to take a risk and let yourself and your work be seen.

We appreciate you taking the time to read this work of art and invite you to share in worshipping the God who has taught us all how to create.

Without further ado, we are proud to present to you the book, Brutally Broken Beautifully Redeemed, and we are honored to welcome Laua Schonlau to First Time Press.

Sincerely,
Christopher D. Stewart
Founder and Owner

Who gave himself for us to redeem us from all lawlessness and to purify for himself a people for his own possession who are zealous for good works.

- Titus 2:14

CONTENTS

APPENDIX

INTRODUCTION

If you've been brutally broken, but still have the courage to be gentle to others, then you deserve a love deeper than the ocean itself.

-Author Unknown

My story is filled
with broken pieces,
terrible choices,
and ugly truths.
It's also filled with
a major comeback,
peace in my soul and
a grace that saved
my life.

-Author Unknown

CHAPTER I

BROKEN

It's Saturday morning.... I am sleeping in. Then, there is the sound of the door handle turning. A sound I despise because I know what is coming. He is there. I hear the slight click of the door as he closes it behind him. I can hear him breathing as he is walking toward my bed. My eyes are tightly shut. I hate everything about being alive. He comes over to the bedside and lays on top of me. The emotional battle going on inside of me is pure hell. I want to cry. I want to scream. Most of all I want him and other family members dead. Please do not do this to me again. I loathe Saturday mornings when we are the only ones here. The sexual abuse never ends. I feel like it never will. The lost feeling and the longing to never be here again is overwhelming. The air seems so thick and disgusting with the scent of him. His breath on me makes me nauseous. What did I do to deserve this? Why can it not just end? The only way out I can see is if other lives ended to save my own.

This was a way of life for me for many years. Many of you have been there, in the same type of situation. The surroundings may be different. The person may be a different family member. Nonetheless, you know that hate, rage, destruction and need to escape. But how? It's the million dollar question in these circumstances that happen far more than anyone knows.

Being shoved into this situation makes you feel worthless. Alone. As though no-one will ever be able to love you. It is not a matter of what your self worth is because you have none. There is no self esteem. I hope you can hear me above your pain as I tell you: You are not broken beyond repair. You are worth something. Your life does matter. You have purpose. And yes, one day, you can actually know what "love" is. You can discover the key to your own happiness/value/self-esteem, etc.

I'm Laura Schonlau and this is my bittersweet story. It is for those who are so broken you live in the state of despair and depression all the time. Those who have that feeling of hopelessness. I know those all too well. I have lived them. And God saved me from them. DO NOT stop reading here!!!

I'm not going to shove God down your throat. I am simply going to share my story as I wholeheartedly grieve for you where you are.

People who were raised on love see things differently than those that were raised on survival.
-Author Unknown

Have I always believed in God? No. Plain and simple. Bottom line truth is I asked Him to save me one time, and he did not do anything. I went home and it was the same thing over and over again. To me, God could not exist or He would not let this happen. If He was so great, then where was He? Why did He not save me like the preacher guy said He would? But wait…. maybe, just maybe, IF there is a God…I'm too pathetic for even Him to love. If I was such a horrible child and unloveable by my very own family, maybe that's why God turned His back on me.

After days and weeks that turned into years of contemplating this, I decided there was no way God could exist due to all the sexual abuse I encountered. My thoughts were "if He was real, He would not allow this to happen".

No, it was not just on Saturday mornings. Those were just the days I just knew would be a sure time it would happen if he was there. He would make it so we were alone. He would lock the front door so my brother could not walk in on the act taking place on this side of the door. How I despised being on this side of the door. I wanted to be the one he sent outside to play or the one he gave a little money to so I could go get some candy at the store. Why was this happening? What made me such an unloveable child that this is what I deserved? Why couldn't they love me like they loved my brother? Why did my little brother have to exist? I fully believed if it were not for him, they would love, care, protect and take care of me...right? Right? As much as I needed someone to save me, I needed someone to tell me 'yes, your right'. How I longed to hear that I was good...

Many of you can relate right this very minute.

My mother walked in on the act one night as he was 'rubbing' against me. I can still hear her saying: 'Are you happy now? Is this what you wanted? Is this how you call him, coming into the kitchen & signaling him with the light from the refrigerator? Go to your room!'

Hmm. I was told I brought this on myself, so many times...so after that I would wear oversized shirts, usually boys shirts, in hopes no one else would do this to me too. I mean obviously it was my own fault right? My own mom said it was. So I was quite the tomboy.

A few of years later, I remember a young girl right down the street from us. I will not use her name to protect her privacy. All of the sudden one day, her and her mom moved out. I wanted to know why. Later I heard about her mom finding out her dad was sexually abusing her and they left. I remember hearing adults say they hoped he rotted in prison and got what he deserved. I was very young. I knew what was happening in my home. I could not help but wonder what her dad did that was so different that it made her mom take her away. Most of all, I wanted that too, but I never found out what the key was or what you had to do for that to happen. I remember wondering if it was her fault. Maybe she did not want to be taught what you have to know for when you get married so you can please your man. (I can honestly say, at that time I did not even actually know what that meant.)

I know some of you are relating to me more and more. Some of you are sitting there in tears because you feel like I am describing you. I cannot help but wonder...did you ever tell anyone? Or did your fear, feelings and lack of self worth take over and you kept your secret hidden...possibly still hidden. Did you feel it was your job to have to protect 'the secret' because you believed it was all your fault? Told it was all your fault? As tears run down my cheeks for you right this very minute, I just want to hug you and tell you have valuable you really are. You are not hopelessly broken, you are fearfully and wonderfully made.

So many women have come to me, mad, fueled with hate and demanding to know who I thought I was speaking to women when I obviously had the good life other women wished they had. When they would hear my testimony of all this, they would break down. Tears flowing like a dam unleashed. They had been sexually abused as a child. Their parents had done/allowed these same things to happen. Beautiful women who felt broken beyond repair. Some who never told anyone, some who told their mother, some who had told a friend and wound up in the school counselors office only to be removed from the home yet your mom stood up for your abuser. Maybe she even called you a liar in court. Only for you to be placed back in the same home for the abuse to continue. These are a few of the stories that have been shared with me. Many of you have never even told your husband. Some of you have still never

CHAPTER 1 - BROKEN

told anyone.

When I think about the statistics on children sexually abused, it is laughable. Are you kidding me? They are nowhere near close to being correct. I read those and get irritated. It's so ridiculous. 25-35% of Women and 10-16% of Men are sexually abused ranging from fondling to intercourse. 15% under age 12 and 29% between the ages of 12-17. Do you have any idea how many people have never reported their sexual abuse? The number skyrockets above these. Many of you know what it was to tell your mom, someone you trusted or have been caught in the act and they chose to look the other way. To blame you. To leave you unprotected. To turn their back on you. To leave you hurt, broken and feeling unwanted/unloved. I know exactly how you feel and I'm so sorry, with every fiber of my being, you had to suffer that trauma.

Of all the monsters I imagined growing up...I didn't realize humans were the real ones.
-Author Unknown

As kids, we were afraid of monsters. They might be in the closet or under the bed. I used to put one foot out of the covers and would eventually put it back for fear something under the bed might reach up and grab it.

A tree limb near a window and my imagination would run wild with what might be outside trying to get in. Nightmares of monsters or scary characters that would chase me and sometimes my friends too. I would wake up with my heart throbbing in my chest. I would be so scared and tried to hide under the covers from it all.

I was allowed to watch a movie about Boggy Creek. Afterwards, I was so scared to go to the bathroom anywhere the toilet was next to the window. I had this unrealistic fear of the boggy creek monster breaking out the window and getting me. We picture grotesque monsters that turn out not to be real. But, in our mind, in that moment…we feel like they are.

Vampire movies always made us second guess if they were real. What if we encountered one of these life sucking beasts? The threat in our mind was very real, if unrealistic.

Our imaginations can run in so many directions at once. A friend of mine was waving to me through a window on a dark night. I couldn't tell who she was & thought someone was watching me. I remember being so scared I could feel my heart pummeling in my chest as if it were trying to jump out.

Of all the scary monsters I may have dreamed up, they did not compare to the real monsters in life. The fact the monsters are those that actually do hurt you is more scary than anything I ever invented in my mind. The people who abuse you. They are the real monsters. They cause us a lifetime of strife and pain. Leaving us with the inability to function with any type of normalcy.

Four years...four years of living with the real monsters and enduring harrowing circumstances on a regular basis. I had no inkling what normal could even be. My life turns out to show it.

By the end of grade school we were going to church. To me, this was the most unwanted ritual and waste of time of anyone's life. It is where I learned about the pretend God that didn't save you from anything. And yet, people kept going back there and giving money to hear all these lies. I guessed it was what made them feel better about themselves but did not understand how grown ups could fall for such crap when I could see right through it. I had no understanding of their teaching, they obviously did not understand it. Proverbs 9:10 The fear of the Lord is the beginning of wisdom, and knowledge of the Holy

One is understanding.

Obviously they had no wisdom or knowledge to keep showing up doing the same thing each week for a God that didn't exist. All they were doing was making the Pastor's richer.

Once there was a work conference and our family went and stayed in a hotel. The next morning it was happening all over again. Many times I couldn't hold back the tears. Even if just 1 or 2 of them trickled down my cheek, I hated myself even more. As I lay there, usually on my stomach, one of those stupid tears somehow made it out of the corner of my eye. Although I just continued to pretend I was still asleep, that single tear made the whole situation ten times worse. Then I heard the door rattle. It was my brother wanting in. I was so glad because I believed it would stop. But it didn't. There was more rattling of the door. As you know, the hotel door automatically locks when you go out. The rattling stopped. I couldn't hear my brother any more. Dang it! Another stupid tear of weakness made a way out of my tightly closed eyes. A short time later, the door opens. My brother had gone and got my mom at the conference because he could not get in the room. My mom came in first, seeing the scene before her, she ushered my brother back into the hall. I remember hearing parts of the conversation. "What are you doing?" "I was still half asleep, I must have thought she was you." Lots of murmuring I wasn't able to understand. This was yet another time I soared with the high hopes that it would all stop happening. And this was yet another time my heart plummeted. All hope dashed against the ground with a violent thrust that felt like an explosion inside my chest at the realization that nothing would change. I was left alone...again.

We moved around a lot when I was a kid. By the time I went into the 3rd grade we had lived in 23 houses. Yes, all with my parents. We moved around some more before I finished grade school. It was harder to make friends and never ones you thought you could trust. Don't take me wrong, I always made friends wherever we went. I just didn't make the type of friends you could tell your secrets to. School - yeah that was kind of a joke. In and out of different school districts, I had trouble with math. In one year I went from living in Altus and being in the math class I was doing well in, to a math class in Mangum more advanced than where I had been, to Gould, who had a math class 1-2 years behind the first math class then back to Altus again to start Jr. High. The last math class I had been in was on a 4th-5th grade level. The school was so small both classes were in one room. Those kids thought I was really smart. I remember being proud of that. Jumping from fourth and fifth grade math to Jr. High was absolutely horrible. I had no understanding of most of what we were supposed to be learning. Even when I asked for help, it was as clear as mud. My grades suffered. Again, it was all my fault. On hearing "We know you're not stupid, why are you not even trying"? I was trying. With all I had, I. was. trying. But in spite of the bad grades, they passed me to the next grade. Sometimes I think my bad attitude played in it. They probably did not want me back in their class.

Chapter 1 - Broken

CHAPTER II
RAGE

As I got older the hate and rage continued to grow. I played sports. I loved sports. It was a GREAT outlet for my anger. Back then the rules of basketball were much different. We were taught to go in for every rebound, get that ball, and come down swinging our elbows so no one could take it from us. It was one of my favorite parts. There was a near violence to it that made my heart so happy. If I fought hard enough to draw blood from an opposing player, I felt my job had been accomplished. Some thought I was a very aggressive player with rebounding.....I was actually full of rage looking for a place it could come out. One had nothing to do with the other yet both had everything to do with each other. Jr. High is my favorite memories of playing basketball. All the running stairs, laps, up and backs, etc. Outlets for my anger. Many times I've wondered what would have happened if I hadn't had sports for my outlet. I was becoming more hateful at home. Rebellious. I began to hang out with kids that smoked and drank. I saw them as cool with control over what they did. I had always felt so out of control. I wanted what they had. I felt a sense of control with smoking and drinking. A sense of having some kind of say-so about my life. All that I was hiding and keeping secret was more than I could handle. By this time, I had realized what had been going on all this time was not about training daughters or preparing them for husbands. I knew what had been happening was all wrong but I was too embarrassed and ashamed to tell anyone. What good would it do? I already knew it was all my own fault, I had been told that! I didn't want anyone to know how much of a failure I had been.

Oh and this whole 'church thing' we were doing?! Are you kidding me? One of the Preachers kids smoked dope and the other one sold it. They were relatively regular in the circles of the older drinking kids. This only proved to convince me without a doubt, it was all a bunch of made up garbage. The special preacher guys kids were worse than me!!!

Our home life was pretty chaotic on the weekends. It was drunken parties either at our house or at the lake. Sometimes the adults would all go to the bar and I had to watch everyone's kids. Talk about disorderly!!

I learned pretty rank jokes from the truck drivers. My friends parents did not usually appreciate it when I would retell them. They were the only jokes I knew. I repeated what I had learned.

Usually our times at the lake were good. However, I remember one year getting the cutest two-piece bathing suit. It was not a bikini, it had a ruffled front much like a curtain. You could see my bellybutton. I do not know how it came to happen, but at one point, some of the men wanted to take pictures of me. To me, that was like Wow! This must be what models feel like. One of my dad's best friends, Benny, took a picture and put it on his visor. He always told me he was going to marry me someday. He was the closest person I ever came to trusting. But not enough. I did not realize most of the photos were provocative. If they told me to bend forward at the waist, I did. Bend forward & put your hands on your hips, so I did. Yes, my mother was there.

We were all staying at the lake that night and inevitably it got late and it was time to get in our tents. For some strange reason, my brother was between my mom and dad and I was on the outside of my dad near the tent wall. Later in the night I was awakened. I had such fun that day…and then, it all changed. He kept placing his hand on my head and pushing down. I was not having that and a fight now kept it from fully happening. This book is not about graphic details and I am not going to go into them. You already feel the pain, brokenness and nausea I felt. You've had those times. And those times leave you with more anger and hate. The rage that bubbles just beneath the surface. It rolls your insides, the feelings of worthlessness rush to the surface and you wish you could do something horrible to your abuser. Those feelings when you just want them dead so you can be safe.

My new group of friends always seemed to have plenty of alcohol and cigarettes to keep us going before school and on the weekends. The numbing of pain from the alcohol was a rather welcome feeling when I would stay at someone else's house or we would sneak out in the middle of the night.

That caught up to me one night. I was with a guy old enough to drive and we were in a Quick Shop. A policeman that was a friend of my dad's saw us and asked me what my name was and where we were from. I gave a different last name and said we were from Wichita or somewhere, not even thinking about the fact I was wearing a Jr High Letter Jacket. (And that Jr High was just down the road from this particular store.) Needless to say, I got to ride downtown to the police station and they called my parents. I remember thinking how weird it was when my parents were talking about me sneaking out the window. You should have seen how much angrier my dad became as I told them I didn't sneak out a window, I went out the front door. I should have just kept my mouth shut. I was grounded forever and my dad planted cactus under my window. It was the first time I had ever snuck out of our house. I always found it ironic to place cactus under my window...I used the front door.

It was so easy to sneak out at friends houses as well. We would always go where the older boys would be hanging out. That's where the beer and cigarettes were. A couple of the girls dated the older boys but I was't allowed to date boys with cars yet. But boy, did I love the muscle cars they had!

I liked boys. But even at such a young age, I wanted one that would love me, protect me and take me away from all the garbage. I truly believed the sooner I got away from it, I would be fine. Those of you who have been through it know....there is no such thing as being fine after enduring years of it. The contempt for yourself stays with you. The self-worthless feelings follow you around at all times, never letting you forget....that you are indeed, worthless. No one will ever want you. No one will ever take care of you or love you. You were damaged goods. How could they? What if you got into a relationship and they ever found out? In our minds eye we believed with all that we were and all that was within us, they would leave us. By now, it's not a matter of low self esteem. Now there's not an ounce of self esteem anywhere to be found. You just feel like deserted wasteland with no purpose. But you fully know it is your job to protect this 'secret' with all of your being.

I remember beginning to start hating my brother. He was in no way responsible for anything but I firmly believed it was because of him, my parents didn't love me. He got to go do things while I had to stay home behind the door. I vividly remember one day behind the closed door...there had been a previous discussion about a shirt I had really wanted but we couldn't afford it. I was told if I was a really good girl and didn't cry or carry on, then I could have that shirt. With that said, I no longer wanted that shirt! How could I? If I ever wore it, I would be sick because I knew what I had to do to get it! It was sickening and I didn't think I could be more sick of the situation!

When I was a Freshman, we were getting ready to go on the Freshman Trip to Six Flags. Uncle Benny stopped by the day before I went and he gave me some cash to be sure I had a good time on the trip. He asked for nothing in return, just wanted to show me he loved me and was concerned about me having a good time. He was the best! I got money for nothing in return. I was euphoric!

By the age of 15, I was dating a boy with a pickup. I loved getting to go anywhere. I didn't care where, as long as it was not at my house. I did not care who we were with or what was going on around us, just as long as I had 'someone that cared about me'. Sure enough, he eventually professed his love for me and my promiscuity began. He had friends that were married and we would go and visit them. I didn't know any other way to express love. I thought sex was love. We dated for quite some time. We broke up when I was at the end of my Freshman year.

Upon becoming a Sophomore, I saw this guy one day. I had never heard of love at first sight but that's what my friends told me I was feeling. I thought he was the most wonderful male ever, anywhere. He didn't have the same feelings for me. He came over a few times but that was it. I was devastated that we wouldn't get together and live happily ever after.

Now that I was old enough to date, I began seeing one of the 'muscle car' guys. That didn't end well. We were going to the quarter mile races in Lawton. We were all eating at McDonalds first. During the conversation, he said something I considered rude and inconsiderate. I jumped up from the table and threw my drink on him. Everyone was shocked and I just walked out. I then went to the races with other friends.

After dating several people, I met John. He was the same age as me so I wasn't too keen on him at first. I wanted an older guy, lol. It's pretty funny to look back on. I liked a guy that drove a yellow charger. He was considerably older than me. He was out of school, had a Dodge Charger, job and house. Once again, he had no interest in me either. John actually wrote 'good luck with the guy in the yellow charger' in my yearbook. John was the same age as me and was also in a couple of my classes. Eventually I wound up going out with him in the summer before my Junior year.

The abuse I endured had continued. There is no way to describe how catastrophic it was for me. Here was my brother being sent off to do fun things and here I was either behind the closed door or sometimes my dad would have errands to run or had forgotten something and would tell me to go with him to get it. It was such an atrocious feeling. I knew what would happen before we returned. I'm not even sure rage is a fitting word of what continued inside of me. I would sit and contemplate how to kill both of my parents. It was very odd because I was afraid of being separated from my brother. I thought I would be put in some kind of orphanage ward with more abuse.

I know. Right now as you are reading and there could be many emotions going on. One of the comments I get most from women: I thought I was the only one.

You're not the only one and neither am I. There are more of us than we would want to count. It's why I know the statistics are so off. The majority of us never told 'the secret'.

John and I dated, had a lot of fun, then he told me that he loved me....promiscuity returned. Shortly after school started, we wanted to get married. In the beginning of the

2nd semester we did. The honeymoon — the most uncomfortable, unwanted feeling...but it was what I was supposed to do. A couple of months later, we found out we were going to have a baby. In my tumultuous and distorted thinking, this would be perfect. This is someone that would truly love me for me. We moved to Texas near his family. At 5 months along, I went into labor and gave birth to our stillborn son. I cannot describe how crushed I was by this. He looked just like John, just a mini version.

In the fall, I went back to school. I still wanted to graduate. I wanted to make friends, so I walked up to a church one Sunday morning and I made a friend who had twin girls. They were so cute. We did not go to church. We walked over to her house and got to know each other better.

John and I become friends with her and her husband. We cooked out and played cards..several times a week. We all got along great. Right after the first of the year, I was expecting again.

As I said, we all got along great. I didn't know we could all get along too well. One night while we were playing cards, John excused himself to the bathroom and my friend went to the kitchen to get refreshments. I asked if she needed help but she said she had it taken care of. Her husband and I continued to sit there and chat. After quite some time had passed, I said I was going to check on John - maybe he was sick or something. Her husband headed toward the kitchen to check on her. She was not in the kitchen, he was not in the bathroom….then we heard noises…coming from the bedroom. He marched to the door but it was locked. They were engaged with one another with us right there in the same house. How could we have been so naive? He and I both broke down right there at the end of the hall in front of the bedroom door. When I gathered myself back together, I took off walking. I walked around town for a while not wanting to go home because he would eventually be there. How could I face him? What was I doing wrong? Why would he do this?...... What did I need to be doing that I wasn't? What was it about me that made me so unwanted and unloveable?

Do you see my pattern? Something went wrong…it had to be my fault. In my mind, I was totally convinced that I was the one that caused everything to go wrong. I caused him to do this. I carried guilt with me for more years than I would like to admit.

The next day John and I were both home. Me in tears wanting to know why he would do this. Asking if he wanted a divorce, along with many other questions. I also kept asking what I could do to change his mind about her, what did he need me to do to make it better. Same old, same old. How was this my fault and how do I fix it. She came over and shoved her way through the front door going through the house looking for John. She finally ran to the bedroom and threw herself across him, professing her love for him. This only made it more humiliating than it had been. She finally left. John wasn't sure he wanted to work things out.

CHAPTER 2 - RAGE

CHAPTER III
A DAUGHTER

Imoved back to Oklahoma. I found a cute little house and John had said he would pay the rent and bills. Eventually he came around and wanted to come back home. Yep, I was dumb enough to let that happen. Then the other woman started calling and he would be gone from home at times for extended periods of time. Then he wasn't taking care of our bills and I wasn't working. Nor did I want to. I simply wanted a healthy happy little girl.

With no other options, I moved back home. My daughter, Jessica decided to come into the world at only 7 months. It was crazy. They medi-flighted her to Oklahoma City to the NICU (Neonatal Intensive Care Unit). They had to put an IV in her soft spot which they covered with a little dixie cup with lace around the bottom. She weighed 3 pounds and 3 ounces when she was born. She dropped down to 2 pounds 2 ounces. My parents would take me back and forth to Oklahoma to spend time with her. She was so tiny. They discovered she had a hernia and needed to do surgery. Get this! Keep her size in mind! Her ovaries were too heavy for the supportive tissue below them so they had to reinforce that tissue. Then they discovered she couldn't breathe on her own so they had to place

LAURA SCHONLAU

a tracheostomy tube. It was just one thing after another and the whole time all I could do was hope she would survive. With the tracheostomy tube she could breathe on her own. Her father never showed up but did serve me divorce papers. He also swore he sent her a 5ft teddy bear and he did not know what happened to it. (Insert eye roll here).

I had mentioned Benny earlier. He was still a part of our lives but had moved to Oklahoma City. During our trips, Benny would meet up with us. We would leave the hospital and go to the movies or find something to do before returning to the hospital. One weekend in particular I will never forget...We (parents, myself and Benny) went dancing. Benny had gone over to talk to my mom and dad. He came back and asked me to dance. During the dance he asked me to marry him. I was in disbelief. He wanted to take care of me and Jessica. I had grown up knowing him as crazy Benny for all of the MANY crazy things he did. I used to refer to him as Uncle Benny when I was growing up. But, more importantly, he had been my dad's best friend for years. I would never be away from them if I married him. What would happen if he found out about my 'secret'? What would happen if I thought my daughter

34

had been touched improperly? I didn't think he could have handled my killing them and still love me. Killing them...the thought was always right there. I politely declined and still wish today I could have explained some things to him. My heart was so heavy for him. He did have the best of intentions.

Now, do not get me wrong here. I was not the twenty-four hour doting mother who never left the hospital. We could not be there all the time and on the weekends we could not be there I would go out to the bar. The alcohol numbed the pain and allowed me to be in a totally different place where I didn't concede to the thoughts that my daughter may not live.

I met a new guy, Larry, at the bar. We hit if off great and loved to dance together. We didn't live in the same town, so he would drive the forty-five minutes to see me. He began taking me to see Jessica in the hospital. The nurses assumed he was her dad since they had never seen her father and that's how he would sign in and get to see her with me. He just seemed so wonderful in every circumstance.

Jessica was in the hospital for just over three months. She came home for the first time at the end of October. Her father happened to be in town and saw me at the store. He did ask about her and if she still had all the tubes and junk attached to her that she had in the hospital. (I had told him about all the tubes, ventilator, surgery etc in the very beginning. That was when he told me he sent a five foot teddy bear) I said no, she was doing fine so he stopped by to see her. He stayed in his truck and I had to take her out to him. He immediately began raising his voice at me for lying to him. She still had the tracheostomy tube. Considering all she had been hooked up to in the hospital, and all she'd been through, that tube was nothing to me. But it was to him. He chewed me out, called me names and he sped off and never saw her again. Never paid his child support or checked on her at all.

Larry would come visit and take us places. I would take Jessica to his parents house. Life seemed good and he loved Jessica as well as me. Eventually we decided to move to Texas for his job. At first it all seemed to be going well. Then Larry would be grumpy a lot and raised his voice to me at times. I was used to raised voices, it was how I grew up. We were drinking too much in the evenings and his continued to increase, which resulted in arguing and fighting. One day he got mad, threw his keys and they hit me in the back. He told me just to go back to Oklahoma, which I eventually did, to my parents house. They allowed it and wanted Jessica taken care of.

Not too long after that, Larry also returned to Oklahoma and we got back together for a short time. One night while we were out, he had too much to drink and began being a complete jerk. Finally he told me that I was being a witch and ruining his fun and we should start seeing other people as well as each other. He broke my heart. I went ahead and went home. Later that night I heard his car. I looked out the window and sure enough there he was. Eventually, I went out to the car and he was passed out. I went to take his car keys so he wouldn't try driving when he woke up. When I did, the whole cylinder came out. I thought that was even better in case he had a spare key! (I had no idea you could start it with a screwdriver that way.) Sure enough, he was gone the next morning.

Then came the call. He was dead. He lost control of the car and hit a concrete barrier, killing him instantly. My whole world shattered in that moment. As if that wasn't bad enough, his family called later that day - his father said he knew something like this would happen with

us running back and forth all the time and I
was not to come to the funeral home, funeral or
cemetery. His father told me it was all my fault. I
could not see any hope at that time. My parents
never liked him to begin with so there I was to
grieve over him alone. My parents had paid for
one of my friends to visit from California. Her
name was Jacquie and we had been childhood
friends until she moved away. She was there
when it happened but had to leave and go back,
so it was just me.

Another sexual advance came. Seriously? I
told my mom and decided I was moving out. I
couldn't wait for an apartment for low income
housing any longer. I needed out. After my mom
and dad talked as I was packing, they informed
me that if I left they would stand together and
turn me in to DHS as an unfit parent. What??? I
was totally blown away. Housing did eventually
come open for Jessica and I, but not soon
enough for me.

Chapter 3 - A Daughter

4

CHAPTER IV
Co-Dependency

I hated being alone. I thought I 'needed' someone in my life. Someone to make me happy. Surely there was a man that could love me and make me feel loved.

A few months later we found out my parents were going to have another baby! What? They had to be crazy. All I really had to say was it will be all right as long as it's not a girl. I knew deep inside, if it were a girl....'the secret' was coming out! I wound up getting another baby brother. Life was good. He was a year and a half younger than my daughter.

Back to the bar I went on the weekend. You guessed it, I met another guy, we fell in 'love'. I moved into an apartment and it was not long before he was basically living there with me. We got married and I was a wreck.

This habit of falling into this gaping black hole was a continuous recurring event with me. The one where I didn't feel good, all I wanted to do was sleep, I didn't keep the house clean and I had no energy at all. I had done this type of thing, even before I was married, several times but it seemed to get worse each time. It wasn't fair to anyone, yet I could not help it. I felt like a loser, I didn't know what was wrong but I had plenty of input about me being pure lazy. I didn't want to be this way and yet couldn't figure out how to stop it either.

Nearly 2 years after Bobby and I married, we welcomed another little girl into our home. Victoria was precious but she would not sleep. She cried all the time it seemed. It was exhausting on both of us. She was a few months old before we were able to get her on any kind of schedule and I use that term loosely. In just a couple of months we moved to Ponca City. We loved to go out dancing and having fun with family and friends which were related to him. After a few months, the black hole was back. Some of you will understand this 'black hole' of mine but, at the time, I didn't.

Eventually Bobbie was coming home later and later, sometimes with no explanation of where he had been. This was taking a huge toll on our marriage. Eventually we were not going out together very often. I would go out with his family. One night I met a handsome young man but nothing came of it. We didn't go out or continue seeing/talking to each other. It was just a great night with someone paying attention to me.

I had taken a job working nights as a waitress to help with our income. My marriage was very rocky and I met a guy after the bars had closed one night. Mark had come in with three or four other guys. We all laughed and joked and they came back the next week. He wound up leaving me his phone number and address. Feeling lonely and jilted at home, I found solace talking to him.

One night a friend of mine called and wanted me to come over right away. She and her husband had gone bowling with Bobbie. No big deal. EXCEPT, Bobbie left with a waitress at the bar and my friend thought I needed to know. She told me that she would want to know if it was her. That was it. I had, had it. I called the guy from the restaurant and cried on his shoulder. He was very understanding, said all the right things and made me feel like everything would be ok. Then I began stopping by his house. Eventually leaving Bobbie, getting my own place with the girls and continued seeing the man that 'understood and cared' about me. In a short period of time, we moved in with him.

So, here I go again! Only this time I had no idea what I was in for. You hear of men being called a 'mama's boy'. Yeah, I did not realize this until way too late. Eventually we got married. He explained to me since we'd both been married before we could just go to the Justice of the Peace and use the money that would have gone toward a wedding on the honeymoon instead. This sounded reasonable to me, so that's what we did.

El Palacio! The thought makes my mouth water. It was a Mexican Restaurant that we went to nearly every week. They had the best chili relleno's anywhere. We used to have a great time in many things we did together. We would ride 4 wheelers and have such a fabulous time with friends at Little Sahara! I loved the feeling of riding the trails, climbing the dunes - I felt free. It was exhilarating!

I got along with his dad and his wife but getting along with his mom? Well, I was trying but she was not very open to it. After we had been married 3 months or so, I noticed he was gaining weight. Eventually, through something his mom said (which I don't remember now but something about seeing him in the morning) made me question what she meant. He had never told his mom we got married! He had been getting up in the morning, eating breakfast, grabbing his lunch and heading out to work. What I didn't know was he didn't go straight to work! He went to his mom's and had breakfast again and took a lunch from there as well. This is what he had done before we got married and if he stopped she would know something was going on. Seriously? I told him from then on his mommy could take care of him! I was furious. To him, he did not lie he just didn't tell me or his mom the whole truth. I would much rather hear truth. A little lie is a lie. There went any trust I may have started building. I was hurt, mad and that darn black hole returned.

When it came to his mom there was just no getting along. When they were together there was no getting along with either of them. It did not help that I was quite verbal and mouthy. He didn't believe he should have to help around the house at all. He should be able to go to work, come home to relax and watch tv then have his chocolate chocolate chip muffin with milk before he went to bed. His mom felt the same way (except for the muffin), so I was doomed. I also worked a full time job, I didn't see it this way at all. Yet, I had screwed up so much with men already how could I leave? So I stayed through the emotional abuse. This only made the truth even more obvious: I was worthless. No one would ever want me. I could not do anything right. All these thoughts were showing back up but even stronger.

Do not take me wrong, there were times we got along great. Around his dad we always had fun - going to OKC shopping, out to eat, when they would come over or anything we did together.... We would go ride 4 wheelers with his friends. However, we did not get along as much as we used to. His mom always had advice for him on how I should be. Sometimes those arguments could turn from yelling and slapping to knocking me down.

I was talking to my mom one day and she said she would be helping her friend out tomorrow. I knew the friend, my parents used to play cards with her and her husband. I asked what she needed help with? There are no words to describe the way I felt in the next few moments that have actually lasted all of my life. She told me her friends' husband was being sexually explicit with her daughter. And she was going to help them out with packing. I truly do not remember what she was saying for a few moments. All I could think was, 'you will go and help someone's daughter but you wouldn't help your own daughter'? This thought stayed in my head consistently for days. The black hole returned. My mind just could not understand

and desperately wanted to. What was so horribly wrong with me?

I had friends (Beverly and Natalie) and they were who I would spend my time with when things were crazy at home. We spent a lot of time together. They were they greatest! Our kids all liked each other and got along. I did share about the sexual abuse when I was younger. I thought telling someone would help to ease the rage, hurt and shame. It did not. They tried to be understanding but those feelings of shame, worthlessness, weakness, and guilt just became stronger. It was great to go to either of their houses when things would be so crazy. But... the black hole kept returning. It just refused to go away. Neither would the rage, hate, hurt, or shame. They were always there. Always close. Always reminding me.

I reached a point of barely being able to function. Of course, Mark was telling me I was lazy, worthless, blah, blah, blah as usual. I talked to my mom about taking the girls so I could go and see what kind of help I needed or treatment, anything to make this misery go away. My family would not help with them so I had to go to my ex and plead with him for help. I didn't want them in DHS custody, yet I knew I could not take care of them at the time. I could barely take care of myself at that time. My ex did take the girls and I went to the Dr., and began seeking a counselor. Upon finding one, I let my mom know I had went and the counselor had wanted to know about my childhood and I had told her. Do you know how well that went over? I can still hear the words so clearly today: 'Why are you always trying to ruin our good name?' I can't even begin to describe the pain that wrenched my heart. Some things never change. I was already fully encompassed by the black hole. I didn't think it could get worse but her words actually made it darker and more overwhelming.

After a couple more visits, the therapist thought Mark needed to come in with me to help me work through this. I thought this was a fantastic idea. I could get better and it could help my marriage!?! Sign me up!!

Not hardly. Mark's response was "I am not taking off work for this crap. I don't want anyone knowing you need a stinking shrink." Trying to explain what I had been through and how this could help fell on deaf ears. Again...pain that couldn't be put into words. The therapist did give me some medications that seemed to help. Then she wanted to do some sessions where I would have to describe, in detail, every incident so I could reach healing! What? Why would I do that? I obviously hadn't done well with it the first time around. I checked with my Dr. to see if he could prescribe the same medications for me if I didn't go back to see her. He could and I never went back!! I also did not stay on the meds once I was feeling better.

When the girls came back home, Mark was a total jerk. He had been a jerk through the majority of it so it was not much different. It was heart warming to know I had Beverly and Nat to lean on.

After being married 3 years, I found out I was pregnant. This rocked my whole world. It was not planned and I had no idea how he was going to react to this. His reaction? Quite classy. "You better hope it is a boy or you will be finding somewhere else to live". I was dumbfounded at this response. I just dismissed him and went on. I also wanted a little boy, we already had 2 girls. It would be perfect.

During my pregnancy, I carried our son very low. It was not long before I was not allowed to lift anything heavier than a gallon of milk. I was considered high risk because I hadn't made it to full term with my other children. By month

7, I had to leave work due to myself and the Dr. not wanting him to arrive early. We did make it to the eight month when Dillon was born. We had our boy! I wanted to have my tubes tied but had a bit of a cold and the Dr suggest I wait. No worries, I will get to feeling better and have it done then. Later I wound up in the ER with bronchitis. I kept going but couldn't shake this sickness. Eventually I wound up in the Dr.'s office because I had horrible pain - it hurt to move, roll onto my side or back or even go from sitting to standing. It felt like I had broken ribs. I had to be carried back to x-ray once I got to the Dr.'s office. A couple days later I woke up in the hospital. Pneumonia in both lungs. One was completely full and the other was eighty five percent full. I was there for just over 2 weeks. At first Mark was mad at me. He was going to have to take care of the kids, etc. and he needed his sleep (insert another eye roll here). My mom came and stayed with the kids to try to help out. He was not crazy about it, yet, he did spend time with me at the hospital and brought me flowers.

Everyone was excited about the baby. The girls loved getting to feed him or help with him. Jessica was nine and acted like a little mama hen toward him. Victoria was only five so he was not as big a deal to her. The moment he started crying or smelled yucky as she called it, she was out of there. They were so much fun!

Once Dillon was born and the holidays rolled around, Mark's mom decided we could come for Christmas but since she had her own grandchild now, the girls could not come over. Talk about going through the roof! I did! I could not believe he allowed this and didn't say a word on the girl's behalf. This caused a major family fight. If the girls' could not go, we would not not be going to her house for Christmas at all!!! How ridiculous! As some time passed, I am unsure what actually transpired between the two of them but she was going to 'allow' the girls to come to her house for Christmas. Like I wanted to go there after all this! We did go. It was strained but the kids had fun.

Things did not improve with Mark. One night his mom was going to stop by. He wanted to know if I had tea made which I did not because I had run out. He threw a hissy fit sister! (in case you're not from the south, here's the definition of a hissy fit - an angry outburst or tantrum.) It was ridiculous! I told him I could run and pick some up to make more. I hurried to the store and got some stupid tea. When I got back, she was not there. I walked in and asked if she had made it yet and he began yelling and screaming at me. Yelling how worthless I was because I didn't have tea. Screaming that she already stopped by. Me, well, being me...yelled back 'then we didn't even need the tea if she was just stopping by' at which time he slapped me and it knocked me down. By now the girls were in the living room, crying and wanting all the yelling to stop. Then he began to kick me in the ribs. Jessica was screaming and trying to get to me and to make him quit. I got up and went into the other room crying with my girls. I couldn't believe what had just happened over TEA!!!! To me, the tea was no big deal. I ran out of tea, it was on my grocery list and I had not been grocery shopping yet. To him, I was an idiot that was not even smart enough to keep the house stocked with things we need. This was the worst it had ever gotten. And again, it was all over his mom. I told you I didn't know how much of a mama's boy he was!

I started looking for a house or apartment. Once I had found one I went to the bank and withdrew enough money to get moved in. I did not leave him totally broke. I am not sure why I didn't but either way, I could leave! The kids and I moved into the house and began getting settled. I came home one day and was starting supper when I heard a lawn mower. Then I realized it was coming from my yard! I didn't have a lawnmower or items to keep the yard up and cared for. I went to the front door and I am telling you, I was shocked!! There was Mark mowing my yard. I went out and wanted to know what he was doing and why!?! He said he saw the lawn needed it and thought he would stop by and help out. In the days that followed, he was very attentive and willing to help me with anything with the houses upkeep. He was very apologetic and wanted me to come home. Needless to say....I did. (Any of you see the honeymoon cycle of this phase? I didn't.)

Because of the pneumonia I had to wait at least a year to have my tubes tied. The following year, I went to out patient surgery and had the tubal done. I was not prepared for all the nausea and pain after the surgery. Mark got more pissed about my laziness and using any excuse to do nothing as he would put it. I took the kids and stayed at my grandparents house for a few days.

After a month, nothing was really changing as far as the nausea went. When I went in for a check up I told my Dr it felt like morning sickness. He and his nurse laughed and he said 'well, we know that is not it'. This continued for a couple of more weeks and I went back to his office. I wanted a pregnancy test done. Something was definitely not right!

The nurse kind of laughed at me and the Dr. told me if it would make me feel better, he would do one but to remember he had just tied my tubes. I sat there waiting for what seemed like forever. The nurse returned, told me to get my things, the Dr. wanted to visit with me in his office. I knew it could not be good. Why didn't he just come back in the room?

When I got to his office he was looking at a file. He had me sit down and told me that I was indeed pregnant. My whole world rocked on it's axis. How? I mean, I know how, but how did this happen after my tubal? He explained I must have been pregnant when he did the surgery but not far enough along to tell when they did a pregnancy test prior to the surgery. I seriously thought I was going to pass out.

I left his office in disbelief. I needed to talk to Beverly. This was not going to be alright when I told Mark. I could already sense the black hole beckoning to me. When I eventually went home and eventually told him what the Dr said, it indeed was not good. He accused me of it not being his because my tubes were tied, (maybe he was confusing it with a vasectomy or maybe he was just so mad he wasn't thinking straight). The rant continued about this being impossible and if it was true he was going to sue. It went on and on. I understood it was a surprise. It was to me too. Eventually we got back to the 'it better be a boy' crap. He was difficult and hateful and I was difficult and hateful right back. Eventually things calmed down for a while.

He took a different job in another town working the evening shift. He drove back and forth each day. One day I noticed some blonde hair in our van. I did not think a whole lot about it at the time. Maybe I had Beverly in the van at some point and those couple of strands were from her. Then I found them in there again. I wanted to know who they belonged to. Of course, he said he didn't know. Then he began to get home later. Then I found them in the middle seat as well as the back of the van!!!! This time I confronted him and was not backing down. He finally told me a gal had started working in the shop and when they got off work they would go to the bar for a drink. He assured me it wasn't just him going, a few of the other guys were as well. Like I was going to believe that. I was very jealous anyway so this really fired me up. Then I spent the next few months wondering why I was not enough. Why he could not just come home? We were expecting another child! Was he planning to leave us? I contemplated so many things during that time. I was making myself sick and began to feel the black hole trying to surround me again.

At eight months my Dr. set a date to induce labor. It was exciting although a bit scary. I just wanted her to be healthy with no problems due to being delivered early. I will never forget the morning I was to be induced. Mark had done some really crappy things to me up to this point but that morning he topped it all. As we were leaving the house, I doubled over in pain while still on the porch. Before I could get to the van, it happened again. I told him that I was certain it was labor contractions. As we began to drive, it happened again. He let me know he was going to stop and grab him some breakfast. We did not live far from the hospital and every little bit I would have that excruciating pain. Apparently due to the pain, I had misunderstood what was about to happen. He pulled into a parking space to go inside for a Big Breakfast. For one thing,

I'm having contractions. The second thing is I can't have anything to eat or drink (which I didn't want at this time but that was besides the point). He put the car in park and began to get out when I asked him what he was doing?!?! He allowed he was grabbing breakfast before we went on to the hospital. I agreed he had said that but, I thought we were going in the drive through and taking it with us. Nope, He went inside. I went in and tried sitting at the table while having contractions at times. The smell of the food, him eating while I was in such distress and people coming in while I was trying not to fall out of my chair was totally overwhelming. Occasionally, I would grip the edge of the table and my fingers would turn white as I tried to make it through the contraction. A couple of people were looking at us. I would have too had I been them! I finally got up and went to the bathroom because I felt sick to my stomach. Once he finished his big breakfast, I was ten times more mad at him than when I realized we were going inside so he could sit down and eat.

The hospital was just a few blocks away but it felt like a half an hour to me. Once we finally got there and we were placed in a room, I was still mad and on the verge of tears. I wanted to have a natural birth. For whatever unknown reason, I never felt contractions while in labor with Dillon. So, I had decided we would try the no drugs route again. Once I literally thought the pain was going to kill me, I began crying and begged my Dr. for drugs to make the pain go away. He made sure I knew what he would give me could stop the contractions. At this point, that didn't sound so bad. It had been five hours and I couldn't take anymore. I was too far along now for an epidural.

He was right. The contractions stopped. It gave me a chance to breathe and get as comfortable as I was going to be able to. Finally, they began again and he delivered little Ms. Shelby Alexis. Once she was born, he asked where her red hair came from. We both looked at him rather quizzically and he said 'don't look at me, I didn't do it' and laughed. Needless to say he had reddish hair. Both of us had red hair in our families so it was not a big surprise. I had a lot of natural red highlights and 3 uncles with red hair. Mark's brother also had red hair. She was just a surprise all the way around.

After she was born, Mark went home because he was so tired. He left a note on the door for the girls not to wake him up and that they had a sister. They were both excited and wanted to come and meet her but knew they couldn't until Mark said so. They were ecstatic to have a little sister.

Once we came home from the hospital, we all tried settling into a routine. Not Shelby. She was also a night owl. Mark began getting up with her every other night. Being sleep deprived, I felt like a zombie some days. On nights it was his turn to get up with her - if he didn't get up when she would start crying, I would go and get her and stand next to the bed with her screaming to wake him up to let him know it was his turn. No, I did not feel bad about it at all.

The following August I began nursing school. Yes…with four children. Truth be told it was five. I still did the cooking, cleaning, taking the kids back and forth to the sitter but at night once everything was quiet, we had a small travel trailer and I would go out there to study. Once I was getting ready for graduation, we had found a house closer to his job and I was offered a job near there. While getting ready for graduation, we were moving. Everything was so exciting but so very exhausting.

Mark and I just didn't seem to ever 'click'

again after the whole blonde hair in the van ordeal. Our attempt at building the relationship vanished. We both worked and went about our days. I became part of the Code Blue Team and felt very accomplished considering I hadn't been out of school but a few months. I loved my job, the people, the families, and the fun we had as a staff. It was very intense, don't get me wrong. When things were getting really intense, someone would do or say something to try and break the tension. It was such a wonderful feeling. At times I could feel the black hole trying to get in, crouching right next to me at all times just waiting to begin to fall over me again. I made some great friends at the hospital and one of them did not actually understand from experience what I had been through as a child but tried very hard to. We became the best of friends. Joni was always a bright spot in my day, especially when we worked the shift together. She didn't understand me staying with Mark and did not like him at all.

Looking back on my life, I kept thinking, 'this is it'? No key to happiness. Does it even exist? My life had not been much better as an adult than my childhood had been. Can this really be all there was for me? What about love?

What about building relationships? Being happy - what direction should I go? Is there truly a right direction or is life just one big failure? I have to find out...I wanted more....but more of what? What did my future hold? What does yours hold?

5

TRADING ABUSE FOR ABUSE

I had a hard time believing this is all there is to life. You just move from abuse as a kid to abuse as an adult? Are others dealing with this or is it just me? I move from bad too worse each time I make a move or change something. Why can't I just get it right?

One day this guy was admitted to our floor. He was attractive, friendly and told me the story of how he wound up in the hospital. He was also very good at paying me compliments. Each day I would come in and I would be assigned to his room. He knew I was married but said he could tell it was not happily. We didn't discuss my pandemonium but we talked about everything else. I found myself becoming more and more attracted to him. Tall, sandy blonde hair, hazel eyes, muscular, strong, sweet disposition and so very nice to me.

One day, I had checked on him first thing into my shift and later he was not in the room! I could not find him anywhere. I was searching the lounge, other patients rooms, our coffee area, the bathrooms, break area...everywhere. I thought maybe he left AMA (against medical advice). I can't even begin to tell you how sick I felt at the thought of calling his Dr. and telling him that I had lost his patient. Later, as I went by his room, there he was! I asked just where the heck he had been. He laughed at me and told me it was not like he left the hospital or anything. I could not believe he was laughing at my frustration. He told me when I settled down he would explain himself. Are you kidding me? You've been missing all this time and you want me to settle down? Needless to say, I did calm down and didn't feel so frantic. Then he explained to me that his grandmother was also in the hospital on a different floor and he had gone to see her. You should have seen how his face lit up when he told me where he had been. He looked like a little kid that loved his grandmother with all his heart and was extremely proud of her. How could I be upset at this? I couldn't. Now he was even more charming than before!

When he was going to be discharged he asked if he could ask a favor of me. I said sure, not expecting what the favor was. Some guys from his crew had brought him in to the ER and he had no vehicle to leave. He asked me to give him a ride home! I had a lot of mixed emotions about this. I was kind of excited but what if he was some kind of murderer or something? My thoughts ran wild before I finally went back and told him, I would take him home. Only to find out he had to go to his job site which was about an hour and a two hours or so, away!!! I wasn't sure which of us was more irrational - him for asking or me for agreeing! When I got off work, away we went. We stopped by Joni's on the way out of town. I wanted to be sure she knew where I was going, just in case anything happened to me. She was getting ready to leave and told me to lock up when I left. I turned to David to ask if he was ready to go and he planted the biggest, mind spinning kiss on me that I had ever had. It was literally electric between the two of us. We wound up hanging out at Joni's for a while. It was thrilling to be with him, exciting, adventurous and beyond all reason. We talked all the way to his job site. A lot of it was him trying to explain his job which was as clear as mud to me. I stayed and we talked some more after we got to his job site. I finally left and I had the most euphoric feeling. I couldn't stop thinking about him.

He called every day. At first it was the hospital phone he called because I had not answered my phone. He knew I would not miss his call on that line. During one call, he told me that he could fall in love with me. I told him I didn't think so. Fall in love with my kids first and show me how you treat them...then, and only then will I listen to you thinking you could fall in love with me. He sent me flowers. I would see him when I could.

Finally one night after a double shift, I got home and Mark woke up. We had some words and finally he asked if I had met someone else and I answered honestly. The next few days were a blur of working, packing, finding a new place to live and moving. Joni helped me get moved. We had the funniest experience trying to move a couch in (trust me, at the time it was anything but funny). We were going up the steps into the house and I got wedged between the door and the couch. I don't even remember what Joni said about pushing that couch on in the house but I do remember yelling and letting her know in no uncertain terms that it was on and smashing my foot. There was a lot of colorful words flying during this. We moved the couch back into the yard, sat down on it and decided we wanted a beer. It didn't seem like a bad place to have the couch at that moment. We could sit there, drink a beer, have a cigarette and discuss people's junk. We were great at solving the worlds problems and had a blast doing it.

We did finally get the couch inside but it was not easy. David drove up to see if we needed help. It seemed hysterical to us as we looked at him, wishing he had been there during the couch ordeal and shared our story. Joni and I always had stories. We also always had drama. Usually just one of us at a time. Other times, we would both have drama going on at the same time and it was fierce. But no matter the circumstances we could cry together and then laugh together. It was a friendship like no other. She knew everything about me but loved me anyhow. I can't tell you how odd that felt or how good it felt as well. I was the same way towards her. We talked about anything and everything. We could always find humor in anything going on around us and laugh. Sometimes we laughed through the tears, but we always laughed.

It wasn't long before the hospital we worked at decided to sell to the big corporation hospital. We had the choice to work for the other hospital or get a severance package. I tried a few shifts with the new company and did not like it at all, so I took the severance package.

During all of this, Mark and I had agreed on joint custody of the kids. We would alternate weeks with them. He asked me to come back a few times but I knew I would never go back there again. We had talked about what arrangements we would have when Dillon started school. I really didn't want him to have to change schools part way through the year. Mark showed up one day and made me an offer. If I would let the kids go to the smaller school where he lived, we could split their expenses 50/50. I agreed, believing this is what was best for the kids.

Then several days later Mark showed up to let me know the house we lived in was about to sell. (Somehow this part of the story made sense at the time.) He had owned the house when we got together. I had never been in any of our relationship for the money and he knew that. He and his mom had talked and wanted to know if I would be agreeable to allowing him to keep the money from the sale, lessen my part of the expenses and it would be my guarantee he would never seek full custody or child support. We would always keep it joint so we both had plenty of time with them. I agreed.

David and I were having a blast. I was running around Oklahoma with him. When we would take the kids to the lake and other places, it was always with music and singing. We both loved country music. Every one of us could belt out every word to Blue Clear Sky! It was popular and David and I believed it was written for us!

It was not too long until David was living with me. That 's an interesting way to put it considering a Tool Pusher in the Oil Patch was not at home much. So, we decided to look for a place closer to his parents which was closer to most of the job sites he had worked. We found a beautiful house in the country and once again, I was a small town girl. Jessica and Victoria went to school in the Cleo-Aline school system. They made new friends and although we lived in the country, their friends would ride their bikes the two miles from town and hang out at our house. I always loved those kids hanging around.

Through this, I need to mention my personal space. I'm uncertain why I didn't bring it up before. I was and still am very particular about people getting in my personal space. At no time, does anyone need to be standing real close to me or touching me in any way. This would arouse a deep-seeded anger and I would get very hateful with anyone who got in my personal space. I am totally aware, this was from the abuse as a child but to this day it still unnerves me. It was okay for David to be in my space. He towered over me and I felt safe, but I did not want anyone else standing too close. Those of you that grew up with sexual abuse as a part of your life totally understand what I'm saying. You want control of who you allow anywhere near you. When someone is too close, anxiety and anger begin to arise. It's a horrible feeling and all you want is away from that person that is too close to you. Others probably will never understand this feeling or the flashbacks it causes, but I do. I've been there.

I told David my past. I did not want to have anything hidden from him. He was wonderful as he listened so attentively. When I would begin to cry he would gently reach over and wipe tears from my cheeks and eyes. Once I was done, he held me so tightly. I felt so protected, so loved and actually secure. Secure...that's an interesting word for me. Had I ever felt secure before? This was new. Then he shared his past with me. I loved the openness and honesty between us. He had also been married before and had gone through a divorce with his second wife before we had met. He had a son who I had already met in the beginning of our relationship.

I had a couple of people tell me David's first wife was really sweet but he was physically mean to her and had broken her arm. Me being me, asked him about it. He had an explanation, so I dismissed it. It was an accident. She and I worked in the same town so, I would see her when I dropped off the child support check but never asked her about it.

The kids really took to David and had a lot of fun with him. We would take them to the park and have picnics, go fishing, camp out, play games and all seemed well. David and I had discussed Jessica's father and the fact he had never been in her life. David told me he wanted to marry me and adopt her. He wanted to be her dad. This was like a crazy dream to me.

I had met several of his friends - all nice and very considerate of me. When they would swear, they would instantly look at me and apologize. One of the men, Eddy, was such a sweetheart. When I was at the rig, he would always bring me coffee. They were a great bunch of guys. He worked with another guy who was married and we became great friends. His wife, Samantha, was a busy mom with four kids at home. We had cookouts and I would hang out with her some when David was gone. I now worked at a nursing facility as a Skilled Nursing and Alzheimer Director, so I would stop by before going home.

Not living in the same town or working at the same job, Joni and I did not see each other as much but we still visited and stayed in touch. She knew she was always welcome wherever I was. She was not a big fan of David's and just couldn't understand what I saw in him. I wasn't a big fan of her man and certainly felt the same way about him. But men never got in the way of our friendship. We stayed friends through some of the darkest hours, always knowing we would see each other through whatever turmoil either of us may endure.

David bought me a beautiful two carat traditional style engagement ring. With everything I had gone through with men, I was not sure about him adopting Jessica. We talked to her about it as well. We decided once we were married, we would have her last name changed to his instead of adoption. My track record up to this point hadn't been good. I didn't want to say 'but what if it doesn't work out' but it was my fear. I was afraid I would do something to mess it up. I always willingly accepted the blame for whatever went wrong.

Beverly and her husband went with us to get married. It was such a great trip! By now, I was getting pretty fed up with David being gone all the time and it would cause occasional fights. I wanted him home and to be a part of everyday life. One day, he left it all. The job he loved, the work he knew so well and all of its perks, to be home. I was so incredibly excited and yet felt guilty at the same time. He took a job near home. He was good natured about it, but he was miserable.

CHAPTER VI

THE BEGINNING
OF THE END

David and I were both jealous. The stuff we had been through in the past haunted our relationship. When I got off work, I was expected to call him and talk to him all the way home so he knew I did not stop anywhere or talk to anyone else. If another guy said anything to me, David wanted to know who he was and why he was talking to me. It was the same way with me toward him. I wrote it off at first. His ex wife had cheated on him. He had come home and walked in on them...so it made sense to me that he was jealous. At first I found it rather endearing. To me, he was showing how much he cared about me.

But the jealousy began to turn into anger. It was the same for me at times. Jealousy reared its ugly head and we would begin arguing again with him accusing me of things I hadn't done. His insecurity (which I had as well) made him question everything and become mean. I was a fighter as well, so our arguments became physical. On one hand I refused to be treated that way and on the other hand, his apologies seemed so sincere I would forgive him. Again, I wasn't able to see the cycle. The fighting and anger, to the blowup, to the apologies, and I swear I'll never do it again, back to walking on eggshells and starting all over again.

One of our fights became so intense, he had picked me up and tossed me toward the bed. I still believe he meant for me to land on the bed but I did not. I landed on the wooden frame of the bed. I wound up going to the emergency room a couple of days later. I had a hairline fracture in the femur. What did I tell the Dr. had happened? That it was my own fault and that I had fallen, of course. I told him I was standing on a paint can and it came out from under me as I placed all my weight onto one side of it. After all, I weighed a whole 118 pounds. I didn't want to make anyone look bad because I was not a good person/wife. I was completely convinced it was all my fault and I had asked for it. It was so ridiculously painful when anything even brushed against my leg, including my lab coat with pens in the pocket. But, David was sorry and didn't mean for that to happen at all. So, I forgave him. He continued to apologize for days afterward.

I would try to be everything he wanted and always fell short in some way. In my mind, if I would not talk to him in a certain way, ask too much of him or make him feel bad…none of this would happen. If I would not make him feel like he was stupid or as though I were talking down to him, it would all be okay. I did not tell anyone because I did not want anyone to know the failure I continued to be.

He knew how much I loved to dance and he was great about taking me out dancing. It was part of making up and his way of apologizing. I willingly accepted this because I loved to go dancing with him. He had a couple of great moves when we would swing dance and that was my favorite!

He went back into the oilfield as a Driller and I truly thought this would make him happy and our relationship would improve. I would go to the rig to see him or take food out to him. The guys he worked with seemed nice enough. There was one of them that stopped by the house once in a while. I wasn't too sure about him because he would also stop by my work at times. I had a whiteboard in my office and every time he was there, he would draw on it or put his initials on it and tell me not to erase them. I always told David when Matt came by. I did not want him to think anything was going on that was not. I did not want to give him a reason to get upset with me. I introduced Matt to a coworker hoping they would start dating.

David seemed happier being back in the oilfield and things seemed smoother between us at first. I remember when my birthday rolled around. I had wanted a goat. Well, David got me one. He had left early the day of my birthday and when he came back, proudly announced that he had my birthday present outside. I went out with him but didn't see anything but my car in the drive. He told me to look closer into the car. I kid you not, there looking back through the windshield at me, was a goat!!! He had her in the back seat and she was standing with her front legs on the console!! On one hand I was thrilled and on the other couldn't believe he put a goat in my CAR!!!! I'm just saying…you can't imagine the goat turds that were in the back seat of my car, nor can you imagine the look on my face throughout this ordeal. To top it off, she was pregnant so we eventually had a baby goat we named Precious as well.

My baby brother would come and stay with us. He was such a delight and the kids loved it when he was there. He loved coming to stay with us just as much as we loved having him. Needless to say, my parents were still a part of my life. I kept waiting for the day I had any inkling of an idea anything was inappropriate with one of my girls....I had horrible plans for them, if that ever happened. I was a very fun loving person, but I still carried the rage from the sexual abuse. I couldn't get passed my past. I had no idea the damage it was still doing to me.

By now, Victoria had gone to live with her dad. She had always wanted to be the focal point in his life. Who could blame her? She didn't get to see him much. She was definitely a daddy's girl at heart.

Our landlord decided to sell the house we were living in. We wanted to buy it but couldn't afford the asking price. It was a huge house on some land and it was out of our reach. So, we wound up going to Oklahoma City one day and saw a mobile home lot. We stopped and looked at some of the homes and I wound up applying for a loan. We found a lot in town the owner was willing to let us put the trailer on but it was just that. An empty lot. So we had to dig all the lines for the home to be placed there. If you don't live in Oklahoma, you have no clue about our red dirt that is actually a red clay. We wet it down over and over. The digging was slow and very difficult. I would try to work on it and when David would get home, he would work on it. We finally got it all ready and they moved our brand new double wide trailer onto the lot. It was a beautiful home with a huge Master Bedroom and bath that included a jacuzzi. I didn't realize there were mobile homes that were so beautiful and roomy.

Although we had good times, we had almost as many argumentative and disagreeing times. It didn't seem to matter what else was going on, we would wind up arguing. Be it over the kids or something stupid. Either way, it stemmed from two broken people with bad tempers.

As I said earlier, David was a very strong guy so even grabbing me by the arm could leave bruises. It was not intentional and he always said he was sorry.

We had the kids at the Watermelon festival one year. They entered the bike decorating contest, turtle races, frog jumping and they did three- legged races together. As we were getting ready for the parade, David's mom drove by with his son. I mouthed off about it and made David mad. David went from smiling to completely ticked off in seconds. He stepped over and put his foot on mine bearing his weight down. When I told him that he was hurting me, he simply continued. I was hurting and thought he was going to break my foot.

We had been having a great day and everything changed in an instant. He wound up making us go home because of my behavior. We were all hot, tired, and sweaty. He was yelling as I was trying to fix everyone some lunch. Once the kids were eating, we went into another room and began fighting. Somehow this had become all my fault because I had time with my kids and he didn't have that kind of time with his. I was furious. Once the kids finished eating and cleaned up, I loaded them up in the car. It wasn't time to take Dillon and Shelby back to their father so we drove slowly, went to the Peppermint Pad in Pond Creek for ice cream and then took them home. They were exhausted from all the events and being outside in the heat.

When I got home, the argument continued. Again, he thought I was taking a jab at him and thought he was stupid. He always told me that I would be his forever. I was beginning to wonder. The next few days were much more calm and relaxed and things were better for the moment.

I don't remember now what was going on with my car, but David was working on it that following Saturday. I took him iced tea and asked if I could help, knowing full well he would say no. So, I stayed out there with him and would ask general questions about what he was doing. To me, this was some quality time. To him, I thought he was stupid and didn't know what he was doing. Needless to say, that's when the fight started so I went back into the house. It wasn't worth it. When he came storming in the door wanting to know why I just up and left, I told him it wasn't worth it to fight over something I did not do. Somehow this was interpreted as 'he' wasn't worth it. His anger took over. I'd had it. I was sick of the fighting, yelling and physical side of all of this. Through tears, I told him that I was done and was not taking it anymore. I told my daughter to get in the car, we were leaving. We went to the Curve to get gas and something to drink. I sent her in to get the drinks because I was still crying off and on, my face was all red and puffy. I didn't want to see anyone and have them ask what's wrong. I knew I would just fall apart and go into a crazy whirlwind of explanation. As we went to leave, we saw someone we knew! I didn't want to talk and at the same time wanted to unload. Matt. It was Matt at the Curve. I had never seen him there before. He came over and very joyfully said hello until he saw my face. He was very concerned and wanted to know what in the world was going on. I started to sob, he was trying to be comforting and I told him here and now wasn't the place or time but that I appreciated his concern. He asked where I was going and the truth was, I had no idea. He asked us to follow him to the lake and we could talk there. He did not think I needed to be driving around in the shape I was in. On that side of it, I knew he was right. So...we followed him to the lake. This began the most tumultuous time in my life. I just thought things were bad. I had no idea how much worse they were about to get.

We arrived at the lake, he turned on some music and handed me a beer. The three of us sat and chatted for a bit. He wanted to know what was going on with David, so we walked down the beach to talk. He was super attentive, agreed with me that David shouldn't treat me this way and just listened. It was totally crazy to be talking to him like this. Tears upon tears kept flowing.

As we walked down the shoreline, Jessica stayed close to the truck and music. At one time he put an arm around my shoulders for comfort.

Then I sat down and bawled. He sat next to me and when I calmed down a bit, told me that he wanted to share something with me that no-one else knew. He said, 'it broke my heart when you married David'. I in no way saw that coming! He proceeded to tell me the story of when he met me and wanted me but I was dating David. It was why he would always stop by my office. He was not interested in dating anyone there, he just wanted to see me. He told me how beautiful I was. Trust me, to think I was beautiful at that moment after all the tears, the puffiness of my face and how red it was, not to mention the enormous amount of snot, was not something I could fathom! I kept asking why? He told me there was a part of him that kept hoping David and I wouldn't last so he could have me. This was information overload for me. I've been sitting here talking about and crying over his friend while Matt wanted me? I can't even begin to describe the confusion and turmoil inside of me. What's more, Matt was very handsome, why would he want me? At the same time I found solace in the fact he did. Somebody still wanted me. Somebody cared about me. Somebody thought they loved me. As we headed back down the beach he pulled me by the hand and kissed me. He told me he had to kiss me at least once, in case I went back to David. Now I was crying out of total confusion. Everything seemed irrational and at the same time everything seemed right. I would not be in this place at this moment in time if I wasn't supposed to be, right?

Before I even continue this story, let me tell you….satan can be a very handsome man. He can be tall, dark skin, amazing blue eyes, long dark black eyelashes - everything you always wanted.

The devil doesn't come to you with an ugly red face & scary horns. He comes to you disguised as everything you ever wanted.

-Author Unknown

CHAPTER VII
THE END OF
MY DREAM
RELATIONSHIP

Matt wanted to be sure I was going to be okay and safe. He wanted to know where I was going and to be able to check on me. I was extremely close to my Director of Nursing at that time. I'm not sure an Assitant Director Of Nursing and Director Of Nursing can't be very close. We worked together like magic. I was planning to call her and go to her house. She knew a lot about David and I and she knew he was physical with me. So, Jessica and I went to stay with her.

I was determined I was never going back. I should not be treated this way and would be better off without him. She was in complete agreement with me and did not know why I had stayed this long. She encouraged me to take out a protective order for my safety. I took a few days off work to try and collect myself. Matt stopped by one evening. I had know idea how he knew where she lived. She had given him her address a while back thinking they might start something up. He stayed the night there. He was curled up next to me, whispering the sweetest words to me in order to comfort me and try to help calm my fears.

Upon returning to work, the shift nurses were instructed to tell anyone that called I was unavailable and only take messages for me. Various nurses came to me to let me know they had seen the marks and bruises I had had. This made me want to cry all over again. They were extremely protective of me and it was exactly what I needed at that time. David tried calling me at work several times. One of the nurses in particular was my mama bear. I knew she would take him on if he showed up at work. She wasn't going to let anyone get to me or near my office.

Matthew would stop by to check on me. He brought me flowers to brighten my day. As usual, he would draw his initials or some little picture on my white board. He was so sweet and thoughtful. He was also still professing his love for me.

It didn't take long until I was staying at Matt's more than anywhere else. I wanted David OUT of my house and I wanted to move back in. He wouldn't leave. There was no police department in that podunk tiny town. The next closest town wouldn't send anyone out unless David was trying to harm me. I was furious. That was my home and I should be able to live there. Especially since I was making the payment. Upon finally talking to David, he refused to leave and said he would make the payment. I did not really want to be in podunk America where he could get to me, so I agreed. And guess what? He did not make a single payment.

Eventually I did see David. He wanted to shower me with kisses and bear hugs and I was done with everything. He wanted to apologize and profess his love for me which all fell on deaf ears. I wanted the house payments made or for him to get out, NOW!

I had finally had enough. He was getting out of that house one way or another! I borrowed a friends pickup, bought a six pack of liquid courage and headed to Cleo. I was convinced if I drank that six pack on the way, I would have the needed courage to stand up to him. When I arrived in Cleo, I went to a guys house that knew Jessica and borrowed his tire iron. When I got to the trailer, I went up to the door and knocked. When he opened it, I hit him as hard as I could with that tire iron. He grabbed the tire iron and we were struggling for it when he said, ' What in the heck did you do that for'? I started yelling for him to get out of my house and out of my life...then I realized someone else was there. Now I'm yelling because I think he has a woman in my house! It turned out not to be a woman at all. It was Matt. I was stunned. Why would he be there? David and I continued our struggle over the tire iron. He was determined to make me listen and I was determined that would never happen. In our struggle I realized I had blood on my hands and stopped to see where he was bleeding from. It wasn't his blood, it was my own from fighting over that stupid tire iron. I eventually let go and he eventually let me leave. I drove home in tears wondering how I could be betrayed by two men at once! A part of me wasn't sure I really hated him. In fact, a part of me thought I had felt love for him even though we were fighting over a tire iron. I wanted to be loved, treated well and cared about....but then again, wasn't that what I had wanted my whole life?

Matt began calling. Well, now I wasn't taking his calls either!!!

Matt left messages wanting to explain to me why he had been there, what was going on and for me to just listen! Later, he came by. I opened the door and let him know I didn't need anyone in my life that would lie to me, hang out with that jerk that caused me so much pain and didn't want to hear anything he had to say. He wasn't taking no for an answer. Matt pushed his way through the front door, grabbing me, and holding me tightly as he told me, I WAS going to listen.

By this time, to say my relationship with my DON had become strained would be an understatement. I didn't understand why she was barely talking to me and when she did, she was short, to the point and would then just walk away! One day I went and asked just what was going on. I had no idea she was jealous about Matt! I never knew she had really wanted to date him. Once again, she was short and hateful. According to her, I always had everything and got what I wanted. After some more time, we came to the agreement we couldn't work together like this and I resigned. I went to work at a Nursing Home in another area of town. I was devastated. Another very meaningful relationship in my life destroyed.

I did hear Matt out finally. He and David had been friends before we ever met. They were both in the oilfield and would cross paths at times and he wanted to make amends. He was scared of how tough David was as well.

Here you have to understand, due to no-one protecting me growing up, I had sworn to myself NEVER would I just "tolerate it" and go on every day like nothing ever happened. I had lived with that childish, self-serving standard growing up. I refused to ever be like that.

I had a Glock 9mm and with all the madness thought I might need it. I always kept it near, just in case. If anybody was getting hurt throughout this ordeal, I didn't want it to be me.

CHAPTER 7 - THE END OF MY DREAM RELATIONSHIP

CHAPTER VIII
THE WEAPONS

Little did I know, what having that gun was going to cause.

One evening David was calling and telling me, he was coming over. Period. Matt started to freak out and wanted to leave. He took my car and left. David showed up and was wanting me to get back home where I belonged. He and I wound up getting into a huge fight. I wasn't going to allow him to physically abuse me, he promised he wouldn't, I started in on all the times it had happened and pointed out that I just did not believe it was going to stop. This really made him mad as he felt I wasn't listening. He asked where Matt was, I really wasn't sure but if I had guessed, I would think he had gone to their friend Rag's house. David left, I bawled my eyes out again. Why did he ever have to be so mean and allow his temper to guide everything. If you could get passed his temper, he was a great guy.

I got tired of waiting on Matt to come back and took off walking to see if he was at Rag's house and get my car back. As I got closer, I could see patrol lights. The nearer I got, I realized the lights were at Rag's house. I got as close as I dared and watched through some bushes trying to figure out what in the world was going on. All I knew was I was not going to go any further and didn't want involved in whatever was happening.

Later, I got a call that the cops had been called to Rag's house. Matt had taken my gun when he left without me knowing about it. Several hours after David left, he eventually did find Matt over at Rag's. Matt had pulled the loaded gun and they begin struggling over it on the front porch. Rag's called the cops. He didn't want anyone getting shot including himself and his girlfriend.

Later the next morning, I walked back over to get my car. Rag's and his girlfriend relayed what had gone on earlier that morning. Matt was hauled off for public intoxication and David was allowed to leave. Rag's girlfriend lived in Garber and gave me a key to her house so I could go somewhere neither of them could find me and get some much needed sleep.

After attempting to sleep, I went and saw David to see if he was okay. I was so confused when it came to both of them. I knew if Matt had been hauled in I wouldn't see him for a few days anyway. All I wanted to know was...where was my gun? The cops had confiscated it and I would have to go down to the PD to claim it.

I had found a cute little cottage type house in Enid and rented it. Now Jessica was going to Enid Public Schools. It didn't take David any time to find out where I lived. He kept stopping by. I didn't want to open the door, hear the empty words of how sorry he was or how much he still loved me. I wanted him to leave me alone. Then he saw Matt's vehicle at my house. His calls were so close together. Messages of loving me and wanting me to come back home. Messages of what a loser Matthew was. I wouldn't take his calls. The staff wouldn't put him through to me at work and it all made me increasingly more angry at him. He refused to make payments on the home unless I came back. That was not going to happen. Especially now that I was getting involved with his friend. Something I had never dreamed would happen. I had never even entertained the thought of Matt and I together. It just seemed to happen.

Things settled back down temporarily. I finally contacted David to see if I could get some more of my stuff. I went to Cleo to pick up my things. David was very considerate of me and very nice at first. Then it started...why was I doing this, why wouldn't I stay, what did he do that was so bad, why Matt, etc, etc. Slowly but surely, tempers began to flare on both sides. Me standing my ground of how I was abused as a kid and wasn't going to be abused as an adult. I did not care what my mom put up with. I was going to prove I wouldn't put up with crap! David was adamant that I belonged with him. He finally just said "If I can't have you, no one else can either"! I couldn't believe he even said it. He grabbed me by the arm and shoved me back on the bed. Of course, I am in tears by now. As I went to get back up he shoved me again but this time got on the bed with me with one arm over me. He was telling me that he did not want me to go, he loved me and I belonged there with him. When I turned my head towards him, I simply said no, that's not going to happen. Pure anger shot through those eyes piercing into me. Then I saw it. How had I missed it?!?! He had a handgun. He put it up to my temple and told me again, if he could not have me, no one else was going to either. Needless to say, my anger dissipated and fear was starting to take over. I was trying to talk very calmly and explaining how ridiculous this situation was. Asking, how can I believe you love me while you hold a gun to my head? He began to break down as well. When he put the gun down, we were both in tears. I was trying to talk very soothingly. I told him neither of us wanted me to stay there because he was holding me at gunpoint. He agreed that was not the way he wanted me either. He wanted me to come home because I loved and missed him. A part of me wanted that too, but tonight was another example of why that wouldn't happen. I stayed put that night and left the next day swearing I would never have anything to do with him again!

I went home and cried for hours. What was I doing? How had all this happened? How in the world did GUNS keep getting involved? I was a hot mess to say the least. I actually considered praying about all of this. Then I thought, who am I going to pray to? It reminded me of that little church where one of their verses was Proverbs 9:10 The fear of the Lord is the beginning of wisdom, and knowledge of the Holy One is understanding. That and John 10:10 The thief comes only to steal and kill and destroy; I have come that they may have life, and have it to the full.

If this was life to the full, it sucked. So... there was no reason to pray. I'd already learned He doesn't save anyone or give them life.

Matt came by to check on me. I didn't know if that was a good thing or a bad thing at this point. One part of me said to stay the heck away from both of them. I wound up telling Matt what happened. I couldn't have called the cops about David, I had gotten the Protective Order but I was the one that went there.

Matt moved in and things were pretty good for a while. He had gone to work for another driller named Joe. I didn't know him and had never met him. I came home from work during lunch one day to drop off some food for Matt and there was a red Jeep Cherokee in the drive. I recognized it as Matt's ride to work. I didn't think much of it and went inside. As I walked in, it was completely dark. I saw Matt asleep on the love seat by the door so I leaned over to kiss him and let him know I had brought him lunch. Just as I was about to kiss him, my eyes were adjusting to the darkness and I realized I was about to kiss some other guy I did not even know! I put the food down and found Matt was in the bedroom. I woke him up and asked who the heck was on my love seat and that I'd nearly kissed him thinking he was Matt. At the time Matt thought that was humorous.

Then one day I found out Matt had done some drugs. Drugs had never been a part of my life and they weren't going to be now. I called

David, told him what I had found out and he wasn't surprised by it at all. He came to see me. Now he was holding me and telling me how unhappy I would be if I kept seeing Matt. Again, he wanted me to come home and continued to tell me that he loved me. He stayed at the house that night. Holding me. Kissing me. Professing his undying love to me. Then I began to think maybe I was wrong about this whole situation. I had never understood how one woman could think she loved two men. It made no sense to me...and now...I was not so sure. I only knew it would be disastrous.

Matt showed back up a few days later, full of apologies and asking forgiveness. I never knew what it was about him that could change my heart so quickly, but he was able to. Full of promises to never do it again, we continued our relationship. We would go out drinking, shoot pool, dancing, etc. But he was always wary David might come in and he was always looking over his shoulder.

Jessica was back home and I didn't feel as much like I was riding a mental thrill seeker roller coaster. Dillon and Shelby were with us every other weekend. Life seemed peaceful again but I literally had a fear of thinking that. Like it would jinx it. I know it was an unrealistic fear, but it was my fear nonetheless. Matt worked nights so there wasn't much interaction between him and the kids. At times he would get hateful with me if he thought I was gone too long (even to the grocery store) and start demanding to know who I was sleeping with. He accused any/everyone. His own friends, the bagger at the grocery store, anyone that might casually say hello in passing or someone that waved when they drove by. We lived in Oklahoma....most people, especially in smaller towns, wave when they go by whether they know you or not. It was not like an extend the arm and wave their hand at you, it was raise a couple fingers off the steering wheel with a nod as they went by! At times he could be uncontrollably angry about it.

Matt had decided we needed a vacation away from everything. Ocean air, sandy beaches and some fun was what we needed. So we made plans to go to Corpus Christi, just the 2 of us. It seemed like a really long drive but once we were there it was beautiful. I love the sound and the smell of the ocean. The seagulls and the other birds flying all around. All the different shells and things you could find on the beach. Wading out into the water, sometimes wondering what it would be like to keep walking out into it and not turn around, but mostly just loving the waves, sights and sounds. The first few days were great! I tried oysters on the half shell for the first time. I had no idea how to eat them so I made this mistake of trying to chew one up. Bad idea. Then Matt taught me how to get one of those slimy little guys down. It was comical.

There has never been anything in the world to me as peaceful as water of any kind. I love the sound of water lapping up onto the shores, or waves crashing...it was all bliss to me. We went for a late night walk on the beach. We had been drinking at the restaurant and I was very relaxed. We finally went back to our room and it was the best sleep I had had in months. The next morning I woke just as the sun was starting to come up. I woke Matt up and told him to come and see how gorgeous it was. He looked out and told me to get my shoes on, we were going to see what might have washed up on the beach last night. I was so excited! I had never been to the gulf, never scoured the beach, etc. We walked a long way down the beach. I had grabbed my jacket and was so glad I did. I couldn't believe how chilly it was. We found jelly fish, a stingray, shells of all shapes and sizes.

Then I found the most interesting thing ever. I had never seen one before and soon realized that if I looked hard enough I found more. They were sand dollars! Beautiful yet delicate. I collected quite a few that morning and was so proud of my treasure. I was going to take them home and find out how to preserve them or whatever it was a person would do with them. We went back to the room and just had a long leisurely morning. This was so different than what I had become accustomed to with Matt. I thought he was actually changing. That afternoon we went sightseeing and stopped at some shops. Later we stopped for lunch and had a couple of beers. What a totally relaxing day. We stopped at the store for a 6 pack of Bud on the way back to the room. I thought it would be perfect if we spent the evening on the beach.

David was mad at me for going. He was afraid something could happen to me. He didn't believe Matt was really changing and believed he would turn on me in an instant. I remember thinking how wrong he was. This was precisely what I needed. I couldn't remember the last time I had felt rested much less relaxed.

The next morning we went back down to the beach to hunt for sand dollars and there was a man walking down the beach, sticking a tube into the ground every little bit. We wondered what in the world he was doing. When he got close enough, we asked. He was getting shrimp out of the surf! Who knew!! Apparently a full moon and cooler weather while the tide is out is the best time to catch shrimp.

Later that day, we had a bit of a tiff. Matt swore I was checking out some guy and sending him signals. Thank goodness we got past that quickly. To me, he had to be making changes or that would have been a full on fight. I truly didn't try to make him feel like I noticed anyone else, so I didn't quite understand the outburst. He just seemed a bit cranky that day.

The following day...things weren't going as well. The crankiness seemed to continue. I couldn't figure out what could be wrong with him. Everything was fabulous to me! We ate a late lunch, Matt got a beer and seemed to be in a better mood. When we left, he stopped and picked up some more beer and we were off to the beach. There were a couple of things he wanted to do that we really couldn't afford and it made him mad. He sat and sulked in the sand while I played in the surf and would go back and forth to lay on the towel to dry off while getting some sun. I drank a beer with him and he didn't seem quite as cranky. We had to make a run to go pick up more beer and Pepsi, then returned to the sand and sun. I was having a great time. He even began laughing at some of my antics as I would jump around in the water, find shells, etc. I was so glad he was finding some humor in the day finally.

As the afternoon wore on, the sun began to go down and it began to get a bit cool. We loaded up our towels and went to the room to change clothes. He talked about going somewhere to eat. As he was deciding where he wanted to go, I emerged from the bathroom ready and waiting for wherever we were going. However.....on the way, things changed quickly. He decided we needed to pick up more beer. I thought we (primarily he) needed to get something to eat first. This got an argument started. He thought I was calling him a lush and trying to keep him from having some fun while we were there. Then he started talking about finding a bar. He said if nothing else, maybe he could find someone who was not such a witch and wanted to have some fun instead of always looking down her nose at him. I was shocked. I demanded to know where this was coming from and standing my ground that I had done nothing to deserve this. He reached over and smacked me right in the mouth for being so obnoxious and always playing the part of someone who never does anything wrong and everything in the world is everyone else's fault. I honestly had no idea where he was coming from, much less how we got to this point. He continued driving while yelling at me. Screaming and asking me if I think I could act like a human for just a little bit so we could go out and have some fun or if I was going to continuing acting like a saint. No matter what I said, he got madder and kept reaching over and smacking me or just punching at me in general. Demanding to know if I was just going to be an overbearing witch the entire trip.

I finally just said whatever, take me back to the room and you just go do whatever you want. Again with the yelling! Only this time he starts in with some crap about "you want me to take you somewhere, I'll take you somewhere alright! Somewhere out to kill your sorry killjoy butt. How about if I take you there? THAT'S where I need to take you." I just shut up. My not saying anything increased his anger. He reached over, grabbing me by the hair telling me to speak when I was spoken to. He pulled the car over, yanking me by my hair while yelling to see if I understood him clearly...all the while his spittle splattering onto me. He decided he could not take me anywhere and was going to find a quick shop, get some beer and we were going back to the room and I would learn my lesson. By now, I'm crying and totally confused. I was not convinced he wouldn't try to kill me with the anger he was showing. We found a store and he went in to get another twelve pack, telling me to stay put with the way I looked with my red face and tears - he wanted it dried up before he got back and for me to be happy, not a condescending witch.

Once he was inside the store, I jumped out of the car and ran around behind the store. I'm not even sure what I was thinking other than I needed to get away from him until the booze wore off and he pulled himself together. There was only a field on either side of me...and a full moon. I was standing there visibly shaking, trying with all my might not to cry...and then I knew he had gotten back to the car when I heard him screaming my name at the top of his lungs. I did not see anywhere to go much less anywhere to hide. A car had pulled in and a woman was sitting in it and saw me. She heard Matt yelling profanities, my name and that he would kill me when he found me. The woman pointed at me, mouthing the words "is he looking for you" and I nodded my head yes. She pointed to the backseat of their car. Matt had stopped yelling and she could not see him. I was afraid he had gone around the store and was about to come up behind me as I took off running for that car. I yanked the back door open and jumped in, laying down in the floorboard. Matt had seen me. He came running toward the car but was unsure which one I had gotten in. He opened a couple other car doors, attempted the one next to us and then yanked open the back door of the car I was in. I was literally kicking and screaming as he pulled me out of that car by my hair. The woman was screaming and now people were starting to pay attention to this lunatic half dragging me back to the car. As he was trying to shove me in the car, he knocked the crap out of me. You know, one of those times you feel like you saw stars. Into the car I went and I remember him speeding out of the parking lot. I had no idea what was about to happen but I was positive it wasn't going to be good.

Again, all I could do was cry. I contemplated opening the door and jumping out. I'd rather die from that than at his hands. I chose not to do that either. I remember thinking/wondering if today was the day I would die. Really, no-one knew where I was or would miss me, much less know to report me missing. Tears fell as I began throwing up in the floorboard. He pulled over on the side of the road. I was prepared to be yanked out of the car and beaten to a pulp right then and there so you can only imagine my surprise when he softly said 'Babe, are you okay'? I was thinking, 'WHAT!?!?! Do I look okay'? I just shook my head no as he began apologizing and put one arm around my shoulders. I was stunned. Who was this guy? He was like Dr. Jeckyl and Mr. Hyde. He got out and came around to my door still checking to see if I was ok. Total change of character. I hadn't eaten much so a lot of this was simply dry heaving. As I began to settle down, and the urge to vomit subsided, he leaned in and kissed the top of my head and began to apologize. We went back to the room. He kept apologizing and telling me that he did not know what had come over him. Later he ran and picked up something to eat. Exhausted, sleep came easily.

Love yourself girl, or nobody will!

-Author Unknown

The rest of that week went well, but I will never forget it although I try. Things were pretty normal (whatever that may actually be) for quite some time.

Several months later, things had been going well. On his birthday, Matt left to go to an AA meeting and said he would be back for dinner & cake in just over an hour….he didn't come back at all that night. By 8pm, I had fed the dog the Chicken Fried Steak and by 10pm, I had thrown the whole cake out in the yard. He had been out with friends drinking and doing some drugs. We got into a huge fight. I had thrown the belongings he had there out into the yard. He got physical with me, slapping me and asking if I knew how much that stuff cost. I didn't care! He literally wrestled me to the floor, pinning me down and screaming, causing spittle to hit me in the face. He put his hands around my throat and started pressing, telling me that he could kill me. While holding me down, he grabbed a butcher knife and held it to my throat, telling me now I would shut up and listen or he would slit my throat for me. Which, now I decided I should do. When he gave his 'explanation', all I could do was agree that I believed it wouldn't happen again. When he let me up off the floor, he wanted to kiss and make up. All I could think was, 'are you kidding'? You just held a butcher knife to my throat, after choking me while telling me you could kill me... and now I'm supposed to kiss and make up? I began considering my options. At that point, I just wanted out alive. I was thankful Jessica was at school. Matt worked night shift so they did not encounter each other very often. Non-the-less, the last thing I wanted was to kiss and makeup. Once Matt fell asleep, I gathered some things and left. I made arrangements for Jess to stay elsewhere so she wouldn't be in the middle of all of this. As for me....yep...I went to David. Even though my mobile home had been repossessed and I had blamed him, he was the only one I could think of. David now lived in a duplex in Fairview. When Matt woke up and realized I was gone, he smashed all of my Sand Dollars into hundreds of teeny tiny pieces.

Chapter 8 - The Weapons

9

MARRYING SATAN

David was so understanding. He helped me get all cleaned back up. I had not realized when Matt had his hands around my throat, he was digging his nails into the skin. David cleaned up those marks and put ointment on them. Then he let me cry. Just cry. Marks on my neck that are now scars that I will always have with me.

That black hole that was always beckoning to me. Right by my side just waiting to take over. It had won quite some time ago. I was living in the middle of the black hole with no way out. Confusion, chaos, no clarity at all, little will to live other than my children, always upset and/ or crying, would rather sleep than function and no appetite. Other than work and the kids, I didn't seem to be able to complete anything, no rational decisions, and I would rather hide from everyone. All I could think about is why I'm so worthless, have never been lovable and deserved just what I was getting. I was always convinced I deserved what I was getting.

Some of you are sitting there thinking, what in the world is wrong with this chick? Others of you are thinking about all you're still going through in an abusive relationship or reflecting on one you got out of. I'm so proud of those that got out. You DESERVE to be happy and you are wonderful, precious and worthy of love. Those of you that are still there…my heart breaks for you and your sanity.

David let me stay there for several days. Mostly crying and sleeping. I took some days off work, I knew I wouldn't be the kind of nurse my patients needed me to be. When I finally went back home David assured me that I was welcome to stay longer if needed and that I could call him if I needed anything.

(What I probably needed was a lobotomy.)

I went back to work which was not comforting. I felt like a target there. If you wanted me, all you had to do was walk in. Which, needless to say, Matthew did. More than once. I finally agreed to talk to him if he would just leave and not make a scene. We were up all night. Him trying to convince me it would be better now. Me crying, not wanting to hear the same old crap and just wanting to go to sleep. Although I was off work the next day, I felt totally exhausted. I didn't even have the energy to resist at this point. I finally just said, it was all alright. The next day, we went and shot some pool and Matthew was the most considerate gentleman I could have asked for. Once again he was working very hard to prove to me, he was going to change. I knew if I could just stop making him feel bad and talk to him better, he wouldn't act this way to begin with. I agreed I needed to do my part to help him be better. Eventually we wound up back together again. (I know, you're rolling your eyes about now.)

Needless to say David didn't understand me at all. The truth was, I didn't either. Nothing about my life had any rhyme or reason. It was like I woke up each day deciding which flavor of abuse or honeymoon phase I wanted today.

Matt came in plastered, stumbling, slurring and angry. I just couldn't do it anymore. I told him to get out. I don't know where he went in that drunken state and didn't care. The next day I went to check out some apartments. There was availability, I took it, packed and moved. I didn't tell Matt where I moved either.

David found out I had left Matt & stopped by my work. We went out to dinner and I finally told him where I had moved to. He came over to check it out. I was very pleased with it. Outdoor pool, beautiful grounds and a semi-sense of security due to other people so near. I had made a good friend at work named Linda. She was great to and for me. She thought I should be back with David though. I hadn't shared how crazy things had been between he and I.

Linda and I would have great times visiting at each others place, doing things together and just being there for one another. David continued coming by. Linda invited us to her house for dinner and a movie. David was so thoughtful of me in every way. Linda was excited to have us there with her and her husband. She kept watching David with me and later told me, I was a crazy fool if I didn't go back to someone that adored me the way David did. He would pick me up and we would go to Linda's or out somewhere. You would have never known we had ever had any issues between us. It was bliss. And then....

Yep! Matt showed back up. I cannot put into words what it was to get totally lost in those blue eyes with nearly black eyelashes and his words/actions so sweet. Needless to say, David and I couldn't agree about me seeing Matt again. I didn't need David telling me how disappointed he was with me. I'd always been a disappointment to everyone, especially myself.

This time Matt came armed with an engagement ring. It didn't take long and I had thrown all caution to the wind. We wound up getting married. We actually got married at Linda's house with Joni's dad officiating.

After a few short months, Matt was coming home late and different stuff. One night we had a date night. After dinner we went to see a movie. I had gotten up to go to the bathroom and when I came back took a big drink of my coke and it was nasty! I told him they must have given me diet coke and I was going to exchange it. He encouraged me to just drink it due to the movie about to begin. I told him it wouldn't take me long, after what I was charged for that large drink I wanted it fixed and went and exchanged the drink. Now I had plain coke! About half-way through the movie I took a drink and again it tasted like diet coke. I couldn't figure out what in the world was going on. When the movie was over I was going to throw it away and Matt commented about saying 'for the price you need to drink the whole thing', so I took it with me. Once we got home he kept telling me to drink the coke. I wanted to get something else due to the taste and he insisted I didn't waste the money. This actually caused a disagreement. I decided I would just go to bed and apparently he did not like that. I was all covered up and comfy when he came in and flipped the light on and told me I was not going to sleep! He actually yanked the covers and sheet off of the bed, threw them in the bathtub and turned the shower on them!! This instigated a full on argument. After a while, I obviously wasn't going to bed so I sat down and we talked. We were awake all night long. He was being very seductive and I was responding even though I didn't want to. I couldn't figure out what was going on and I wasn't feeling right. My head was spinning, it looked like items in the picture on the bedroom wall were realistically moving. It was like the guy by the bull was actually walking him down the road and there was activity in the surrounding scene. I started feeling sick. I had to work the next day. I had changed jobs and was doing Agency Nursing. Matt got ready to head out the next day and I was planning to get some sleep before going into my shift. He laughed and said, "I can promise you...you are not going to sleep". I simply said "just watch me! I am beyond exhausted". I was not able to fall asleep. I felt fidgety and would swear the scene in that picture was actually moving. I eventually gave up, showered and got ready for work. I still wasn't feeling well but couldn't leave them short a nurse, so I went in. Maybe an hour into the shift, my heart was beating too fast and I felt short of breath. My pulse was almost 200 and my blood pressure was a bit elevated. The other nurses told me to go get checked out in ER. I told them all I wanted to do was go home and lie down. They found another nurse to cover the rest of the shift and I left. Once I was home, I felt a little better and was convinced I needed some sleep. It would not happen. For the life of me, I still couldn't go to sleep. When Matt returned I shared what had happened. He said he was not surprised but yet kind of was, considering I didn't even drink half of my coke the night before. I did not know what he meant and didn't care, all I wanted was to rest. I called in for my shift for the following day because none of this looked promising. I brought up going to the ER and see if they could figure out what was wrong. Matt assured me, Dr's were not going to be able to help me, I had not slept, stayed up all night and I would be able to sleep after we ate and settled down. I was so thankful he was right. I slept until almost noon the next day.

Once I felt better, day to day life carried on pretty uneventful. Thank goodness. It was getting close to time for Jessica's graduation and we were driving down the road when Matt saw his driller and we pulled into the parking lot. Matt wanted to wait on him and talk to him for a minute. I did not care either way. I was on a day off, we had gone and shot some pool while having a few beers. As his driller, Joe, came out of the store Matt motioned for him to come over to the car. He was closest to the passenger side and came over to that window squatting down to visit. I did not think a thing about this at the time. It seemed innocent enough to me. When we left, I told Matt, I had only seen Joe a couple of times and they were always from a distance but he cleaned up pretty good considering Matt had told me that he was a total lush who drank from sun up to sun down. We did not even get out of the parking lot and Matt was yelling, wanting to know when his driller and I had started sleeping together!! He squealed out of the parking lot rambling and yelling like he was crazy and told me now he was going to teach me a lesson. He said he hoped sleeping with his driller was good because he would kill me for it. He grabbed me by my hair and kept yanking at it. While this is going on he asks me if I remember a particular pond we had fished before. I said yes. I was informed it was a good thing because that's where he was going to take me, drowned me and leave my dead body - that way the animals would get to me before anyone could find me. He pulled over to a little Quick Stop out on thirtieth street and told me not to go anywhere and to clean up my face. He said he was sick of my tears and that I had brought this on myself. He went in the store, I jumped out of the car and was running as fast as I could toward the highway. I needed help and I needed to get to someone, anyone, that could help me. He had seen me bolt and was hot on my heels. I made it as far as a huge ditch that was next to an on ramp but I didn't get that far from him. He hit me from behind, knocking me down and the fight was on. I was determined I was not going anywhere with him and he was determined I was. Here. We. Go. Again. He's bodily carrying me back to the car. Several people are standing around watching but no one is helping me or calling for help! I could hear a couple guys laughing as Matt would open the car door and I would kick it back shut before he could shove me into it. He eventually turned around and basically backed me into the car, smacking me to make me calm down and get in the car right. As he was trying to shove me in he hit my head against the top of the door. It stunned me and threw me completely off balance. He yelled for one of those guys to not let me open that door while he got in. He raced away from there heading out of town. He took me to the pond and told me to get out. I was not just going to get out of the car like we were there for a leisurely day! He yanked my door open, grabbed me and pulled me from the car. Then he asked me why I have to do this kind of stuff? Why I have to make him so mad? Why I'm determined to make him jealous knowing I'm going to set him off? I was silent at first. I had not done any of those things. It was all in his head. I could not say that though so I began to apologize for making him feel that way. He eased his grip on me and began calming down. He did let me know how easy it would be for him to drown me and no one would find me for a long time, if ever. He began to apologize. Here we go again, I knew tears would follow and the begging of forgiveness and making me promise I would not make him have to do this again. Once he took me back home, he went to one of his friends house to drink. I was so relieved. He was on some days off and truthfully I hoped he would pass out while he was over there and not come home.

Jessica was near graduating High School

and I was ecstatic for her! We had a great week leading up to graduation. My parents and Joni attended. Afterwards Jessica went to her graduation party and we stopped by the Quick Shop. While inside Joni said, why are we here? Lets go to Sonic and get drinks there, so we did. Joni went home later and it was about time for Matt to be getting in. By the time he got there he was livid. He demanded to know where I went out drinking and blaming Joni for it. I told him we did not go out drinking and wherever he was getting his information, it was wrong! He accused me of cheating on him and wanted to know just who I was sleeping with. It didn't matter what I said, he called me a liar. Finally, he told me when he stopped at the Quick Shop he asked if I had been in and the clerk told him Joni and I had been in but went out for drinks instead of buying anything. He never did believe me that I did not go out that night. It was total chaos. A storm came in and we were in a tornado alert. Jessica and her class were moved to a Safe Room. Matt finally fell asleep. I went and got Jessica the next morning and couldn't wait to hear all about their night! I was the proudest mama of all!!

After Matt woke up the next day, he

demanded I was to never be around Joni again. He was still insisting we had gone out. He accused me of having someone on the side, then he decided it was all Joni's fault because she didn't like him, etc. etc. I was so glad to see him leave for work so I didn't have to hear it anymore! When he got home, he still was not done complaining and pitching a fit about it. He sat down to eat and finally I told him that he needed to get over it. I had not done anything wrong. It was Jessica's night and I enjoyed every minute of the entire day and evening with her! As for Joni and I, we had gone to Sonic. End of story. Nothing more, nothing less so just shut up. Let me just say...shut up was the wrong thing to say. He jumped up from the table, furious with me and knocked me down. When I started to sit back up he actually took his plate with the food still on it and begin smearing it on my face and head. I was beyond pissed, jumped up and grabbed the phone to call the cops, have him removed and get him out of my life for good. He yanked the phone cord out of the wall and tore off the connection that would plug it back in. He yanked me by the arm toward the door with me yelling I was not going anywhere, he was getting out of my life for good. He had opened the door and turned to look at me, simply saying, 'you think so'? He picked me up and carried me to the railing (we lived on the 2nd floor) and told me it was all over now and began to try throwing me over the railing. As he's doing this, he says, 'you weren't even smart enough to figure out I put something in your drink. You are such a loser and really death is too good for you...but I told you so'. I was grasping at any and everything when it dawned on me to start screaming. As I began screaming for help, he put me down, darted into the apartment and then came running out the door passed me. It dawned on me what had just happened. He had run in the house grabbing my car keys off the table and was about to leave in my car! I took off after him but finally came to my senses to realize to ring doorbells and beat on doors so someone would call help for me. I ran downstairs to the parking lot and he was already in my car. I was yelling at him to take his own car and get out of mine! He started backing out and I stepped into the parking lot. He floored it. I absolutely could not believe it. He clipped me with the drivers side front end. I fell back to the ground and he careened out of the parking lot. I went back up to my apartment and sat down in the floor trying to see if I could figure out how to fix the phone so I could call the cops. As I am sitting there, a total mess with food in my hair, bruising on my arms, my lip busted and looking like quite a fright someone knocked on the screen door. It scared me horribly because I thought he was back. It was two police officers who came in to see what was going on. Another police officer showed up. Before it was over, I had five policemen there and I was the happiest I had been in a long time. I explained what happened. They could see by my looks I was telling the truth. A neighbor had called to report the disturbance. I never knew which neighbor called, but I will always be thankful for them. The policeman put out an APB on my car. Another one fixed my phone for me. While three of them were still there talking to me about how and what had happened, the phone rang. As it began to ring they told me not to tell him they were there. I was to hear him out while they listened. Of course, it was 'baby I'm so sorry, I didn't mean it, blah, blah, blah and I just want to come home. Did you call the cops on me or are they there? I looked at one of the policeman and he shook his head no. They had me ask him where he was. He was at the Quick Shop next door to the apartment complex. One cop was radioing out about it while another was asking if I had somewhere safe to go. I had nowhere that he wouldn't look for me. They told me to keep all the lights off, doors locked and they would let me know when they caught him. About thirty to forty minutes later, a flashlight began shining in the front window of my apartment. I was convinced if it was him and if he got in, this time he would kill me. I sat quietly in a corner crying softly. Then I heard a voice and a rap on the door. The voice was saying he was the police and I could open the door. I was not entirely sure I trusted that. What if I opened the door and it was really Matt? The voice rang out again saying they had caught him and it was safe to open the door now. I peeked out the window and saw two of the police officers, so I opened the door. They explained he had left the Quick Shop before they got there but had returned and was on the pay phone again when they pulled in. They let me know, he was headed to jail, the state would be pressing charges against him and I could come down and get a Protective Order when the courthouse opened. Needless to say...I did not sleep that night.

The next morning I received a call bright and

early. It was the District Attorney wanting me to come to the courthouse in case they needed me to testify. He assured me there was enough evidence from the police involved but the judge may want to see my bruises and possibly hear the story from me. I told him that my car had been impounded because that's what Matt had been driving. He was sending someone to pick me up. When I got in the car, the gentleman driving said, you look much better than I had thought you would after reading the reports from last night. I smiled, thanked him and told him makeup could do wonderful things and many of my bruises weren't visible. He escorted me to the District Attorneys office where I waited while Matt was in court. I got my Protective Order. However, while I am sitting there, Matt comes walking through the door! I nearly fainted. He just looked at me and smiled. The Assistant DA came and got me, thank heavens. I was so thankful for all the police officers and the DA's Office had done until I found out I had no way home!!! I had no words. Surely this kind of thing could only happen in Enid, OK! Well, I actually had a lot of words but none I needed to be saying at the time. I left the courthouse, walked down the street and called

Matt's mom to give me a ride home. I explained to her what had gone on and my next step was to divorce him, asap.

Later that day I received a call from some guy looking for Matt. I wasn't nice at all. I told him that Matt's sorry butt was in jail and if he wanted him then he could go and get him because personally I hope he rotted there and I hung up!!

A few hours later, the same guy called back. I let him know I was not kidding and Matt would never be back at this number or residence again! The voice on the other end said 'I know, this is Joe and I was actually just calling to check on you and see if you were okay'. That made me settle down and stop being so hostile. The guy let me know he was Matt's driller and he wasn't going to get him out of jail either. I told him I was fine now and the longer they kept Matt the happier I would be. He simply said ok, he just wanted to check on me. We talked about the charges and we hung up. How ironic! The same guy that nearly got me killed for something neither of us had done called to check on me. In a way, it was a little humorous.

Start over, my darling. Be brave enough to find the life you want and courageous enough to chase it. Then start over and love yourself the way you were always meant to.

-Author Unkown

Once I had gotten rid of Matt, I realized he had been pawning some of my things. The two most important to me were my two carat diamond ring and my Glock 9mm. No way to get them back. Between alcohol and drugs (he apparently never quit doing), he sold some of my most precious possessions to support his habit. I hated him for doing it but I was grateful he was gone.

Joe called back. This time we talked for a very long time about what had gone on with Matt and how he wound up in jail. Joe was very genuinely concerned, sweet, funny and easy to talk to.

By this time I had decided there was no key to happiness. Building a good relationship had to be a farce. Is this all one big joke or something cruel of the universe?

CHAPTER 9 - MARRYING SATAN

CHAPTER X
A NEW
BEGINNING

If being successful at a relationship is a sign you're doing something right...I may always be wrong. To this point, I don't even see the point. Maybe I never did. All I have really seen so far...is monsters. Is everyone a monster just waiting to hurt/abuse you?

Joe wound up calling and asking me to dinner. He was a little closer to my height, dark complexion, blue/green eyes with dark lashes, muscular, broad shouldered and very well built. We went out and had a great time. No bull, just fun. Joe was on a bowling league and I liked to bowl. I was not so great at it but I enjoyed it. I did not know what to make of him. He opened doors for me, always paid, a gentleman in every way.

Of course, David heard what had happened with Matt and gave me a call. I saw him a few times. But my thoughts were on Joe and why he would treat me so well when we were together.

Joe would take the kids and I out. We always had a great time. Joe's natural demeanor was very laid back. One day we were at Sonic and I reached for my purse to pay for the kids stuff and Joe playfully slapped my hand. Shelby immediately sat up on the edge of the seat and said 'mom, did he just hit you'? Joe and I laughed and explained the difference in someone hitting you and what he had just done. He had done it playfully because he was not going to let me pay. She sat back, satisfied all was well.

However, it was in that moment I realized how much she knew that I thought she was unaware of. She was only six. It broke my heart. You think they don't know...but they do!

Joe was just too good to be true. It really made me nervous. So...I stopped seeing him. I wouldn't take his calls or answer the door when he would stop by. I went back to going to the bars with friends when the kids weren't there. Jessica was gone to Basic Training and was in South Carolina. I met a guy named Rusty. Nice guy, a bit younger than me and he had a good job. David would still pop in once in a while. Life was so much easier without Matthew in it.

After some time had passed, I kept thinking about Joe. He was super sweet and the truth was that I missed him. One evening, I got in my car and went to find him. He was working on his Jeep. I apologized for being a butt. We spent some time together later that evening just talking. I explained why I had done what I did. He acted as though he understood although he thought I deserved someone that would truly treat me well. That sounded good, but had never happened up to this point. These were words I was all too familiar with.

We started dating and had a blast. Bowling, county fairs with all the rides, taking the kids places, taking them to bowl as well and we were all loving it. We could sit and talk for hours. We talked about everything. He worked days now so we got to see each other just about every day. The kids were thrilled with him. About this time a song came out that always made me think of Joe and reminded me of his kindness - a country song about the Chain of Love. At the end she says 'I love you Joe'. This song played a lot!! Driving home one night it came on and I realized I loved everything about Joe and it became my 'Joe song'. I was falling in love with Joe. But it was so different and foreign to me.

The fact I was told Joe was a lush still made me nervous. One of his friends called one evening and wanted to know why I chose Joe. He asked if were seriously dating and told me Joe was a big drinker. To this point all I have ever seen him drink was sweet tea when at my apartment. I found it most ironic that his friend that had called told me that he had drank a fifth and had started another bottle to get the courage to call and ask me out.

When Joe and I would go bowling, we would get a pitcher of beer while bowling but still no sign of what I considered a lush to be.

One night Joe and I sat in the floor near a coffee table in the living room and we were just talking in general. I told him what had been shared with about his drinking.

He sat quietly for a few moments and then shared he had spent a few years living on a liquid diet., meaning he drank the majority of the time. I was a little stunned as well as scared. I did not want to get involved in that as a lifestyle. We talked more about it and I shared my feelings concerning the drinking.

He shared with me about working on the rig, all he was surrounded by and how easy it was to change to a lifestyle of drinking around the hours he kept. He worked on a drilling, which I learned a lot more about. Working daylights had him leaving for work early in the morning (like three and four am) and getting back around five pm or later. Someone always had beer and Joe paid for plenty of it himself. He shared how his life just kind of blurred into one day after the next.

Finally he shared with me how he had quit

all that because he wanted to date me and knew I would never get involved with someone who drank all the time and how it motivated him to quit. I had questions: was he an alcoholic, could he actually overcome drinking so much, was quitting to date me a good enough reason for him to quit and would that last?

We discussed those questions at length. Ultimately, I knew I would know if he was actually staying away from the beer over time.

He did exactly what he said he would. I would send meals and sweets with him and he put on some weight very quickly. He needed to gain the weight and would tell me it had been a long time since he felt happy and healthy.

After a couple of months I was wanting away from my apartment. I just wanted to be where Matt could not find me. He would still call and want to 'come home'. I found a house in the country. It was perfect! It even had a picket fence all the way around it. I told Joe about it and he went with me to look at it and talk to the rental company. He wound up giving all his information too. We got the house and moved in. The house was large and had a HUGE patio. It was perfect for all the grilling and playing outside we did with the kids.

Joe worked seven days a week so it did not leave much time for him to clean out his house so I went and did it for him. Women are generally better at cleaning anyway. I had a trash bin outside, filled it quickly and got it all taken care of.

We began bowling on leagues together. We had so much fun. Every time I would go up to bowl, he would give me pointers and when I was done I always walked up to him and turned around because he would stand behind me with his arms around me. It felt so good. He wasn't frustrated with me all of the time. Things I said never set him off making him mad or hurting his feelings. If anyone yelled it would be me. I grew up with yelling, to me, it was normal. I had a temper but Joe was able to handle me and get me to settle down. We got Joni and her husband Jack into bowling with us. We loved to go to Colorama and Glow in the Dark bowling. They did not bowl league with us but we had loads of laughs. We would go out to eat, then bowl, and have a blast.

I learned a lot about bowling/how to bowl. I also learned when men would say it's a 'man's game' when a woman was bowling or had a woman on their team, I took it as a personal challenge. The good news was every time it would happen I would always bowl over 200.

One of our leagues was the 'Vegas League' and we won a spot to go and bowl in National's in Las Vegas. One of the men on our first opposing team was rude to and about women. I bowled two of three best games I had ever bowled with the first game being a 242. Out of two hundred teams, we took 6th place. It was such an exciting time!

We would drink while we bowled. Joe always knew I had had enough when I would hold up my glass and yell "Mo tea"! to the waitress. Joni and I were always fun to be around but when we were out, we were a hilarious duo!

The following year my grandfather called me and had found out about the sexual abuse. He wanted to press charges. He was telling me to write down every experience I could remember, the year if possible and he was going to an attorney. First off, reliving it after all these years seemed brutal to me. (What you have to try to understand here is in one way or another I would relive it every day. PTSD at its finest. Try to force me to do something, rage would ensue. Stand over me, back me into a corner, make me feely completely vulnerable, touch me and the list goes on). Secondly, I believed too much time had gone by for anything to be done. Lastly, if we were not going after both of them, I did not want to do it at all. To me, my mother was more guilty than my father. She allowed it. We did not pursue anything due to statute of limitations in Oklahoma but I had wished it had been in time. I found solace in knowing he wanted to take up for me. At least one person in my family was willing to stand up for me. The only one, but it was one.

Joe and I were together when this conversation took place and I told him there were a couple of things he might not understand about me and this situation but he needed to know. Although I was still in contact and visited with my parents, I was waiting for one tiny inkling of an idea any of my children might have even been touched wrong. The rage within me was so great, I already knew what I planned to do. Give me one iota of a reason and there wouldn't be a long enough drive to remotely make my anger die down. When I got to their house, whoever answered the door would be the first one I would blow away, then do the same to the other. At that time, I would go sit on their front porch, have a couple cigarettes, then call the police. It would all be worth it to me, regardless of the outcome. I shared with him that this was the main reason I referred to myself as Sybil at times. Joe was as precious as ever and understood in the best way he could as he held me tight and kissed my forehead.

That darn black hole...the black hole hadn't disappeared. It was still there. Calling to me stronger at some times. I had no reason to be sad but I would fall into slumps of sadness and tears. I was always tired, daily functions almost impossible and life was just there. I wasn't living it, I was existing. I had stopped agency nursing and was now the Family Liaison for those in the nursing home from eight to four, Monday - Thursdays. I loved my job but still had the black hole...always beckoning me in some way. Sadness, tears, second guessing, overthinking, insecurity, imagining the worst...they were all with me, waiting to surface all the time.

Joe and I married the following year. A storm blew in and the tornado sirens were going off, it was crazy for a little while. Guests were all calling to see if we were still having it or what the tornado plan was. We had one! If all else failed, we would move everything into the basement. It blew over and had settled down by the time photographer arrived. It was still a bit windy but all else was calm. We had family and friends there but Joe and I were totally lost in one another. It was a beautiful ceremony in our backyard. When our wedding song - Amazed - played I thought we were both going to cry. At least this time the tears would be tears of joy. Instead we softly sang it to each other. His aunt told his mom that she just wanted to find a man that would look at her the way Joe looked at me. Joni was my Maid of Honor and Jack was the Best Man. Dillon was the ring bearer and Shelby was our flower girl. We had another couple we bowled with that helped at the welcome table and as an usher. After the ceremony, we all danced and Joe and I were on cloud nine.

When we arrived at our hotel (still in our wedding attire) we got to our room and as Joe went to unlock the door these 2 women were running down the hall yelling, "stop, don't do it, don't go in there". I looked at Joe and said "someone you know:? He said "no" and we both just stood there as they ran up to us. They were with the Elks lodge and wanted us to come to their party so they could celebrate us. It just seemed so bizarre. We conceded and followed them down the hall. They welcomed us, got us drinks and one of the ladies wanted to sing a special song for us on our special day. We took the dance floor, just the two of us and danced as she sang to us. At the end of the song, a lady came up and put her hand on Joe's shoulder and was whispering into his ear. He looked down and she slid money into his hand! I was furious! What did she thinking she was doing? I stepped up to Joe and said "Did she just give you money"? He said "yes" and I told him to "give it back"! I didn't know what she thought she was doing or getting but she was wrong!! Joe laughed and explained they had passed around a donation plate during the song and they wanted to bless us with the money they had raised to go toward our honeymoon. I felt so foolish and yet why would they do that for us? They invited us to stay a while longer and celebrate. All was good until....the little bald man with no teeth stepped up in front of me and yelled 'it's time to Kiss The Bride'! I grabbed Joe's arm and told him it was time to go!!

When we got back to our room, Joe uncorked the champagne. I got amazing pictures of it. From the moment the cork came out to it lifting in the air, just as it hit the ceiling and it's descent. Those pics are so much fun to look back on. We don't know the people in the pictures from the Elk's lodge but there are a ton of fond memories of them.

The next day we went to pick up our rental car. When we arrived no one was there. We were calling the office number and no answer. The hours on the door stated they were open until noon. A lady from a travel agency came out and asked if she could help. We explained what was going on and she invited us into her office and she tried making some calls to help us to no avail. We hung around for about an hour, decided we were stuck in Oklahoma City for the weekend until the rental agency reopened on Monday. We went back to the hotel we had stayed the night before and they were able to accommodate us for the next 2 nights.

Sunday morning rolled around and we decided to go to my brother's church. I wanted to show Joe off. My brother called us up to the front and prayed over our marriage. It was a bit embarrassing but long term would play a vital role in our marriage. During service, it was just gut wrenching. I cried and couldn't figure out why I have never been able to 'get it right'.

The next day we got our rental car and headed for San Antonio! Neither of us had been there and we couldn't wait to get to the River Walk. All was great, and then....One evening we're walking down the River Walk, holding hands and a woman walks by. My husband is looking at her and says: 'Stay right here, I have to catch her'. The he took off running in the same direction the woman went. To say I felt defeated is putting it mildly. Did my husband actually leave me standing here, while we were on our honeymoon to chase another woman down the river walk?? I took a seat and ordered us drinks while waiting on him. He probably wasn't gone as long as it felt like, but the longer he was gone, the more I could feel anger rising. Eventually here he comes back, steps up to my chair and kisses me on the cheek while I am wanting to know what he is doing chasing some woman down and if he knew her!!!! To my total amazement - He laughed. I could not believe it. I'm rather upset and he laughs! He replied 'she had something I wanted for you' and extended a long stem rose. All frustration gone, followed by a passionate kiss. He was such a keeper.

The next morning we woke up to the 9/11 tragedy. Everyone was glued to their televisions that day watching in disbelief as the scene unfolded. The whole day, everyone's world was rocked.

We spent the whole next day at The Alamo. I'm quite certain we could have gone back for another day there as it was so interesting.

We had a blast in San Antonio and then went on to Port Aransas. The beach, the smell, the birds….it was all exhilarating! We played in the sand and the surf and just laid out in the sun enjoying one another. We went shopping and just enjoyed every second of being together. Seafood, piers, the Gulf, birds, shopping and napping in the sun. It was perfect.

CHAPTER 10 - A NEW BEGINNING

11

CHAPTER XI
THE BLACK HOLE

The following months went by smoothly. In June, the black hole was so close to me. Crying at times for no reason. Fear of going to work started arising. I had no reason to fear work. I worked in a fabulous place. Fears of Joe running around on me. It was just getting more and more out of control.

The end of June the black hole was winning against my will. We had not even been married a full year and living with me really was like living with Sybil. My work offered counselors at no charge, so I went to see one. They referred me out to a therapist. It did not matter. I did not really care what they wanted to do, I just wanted to go home and cry. I ended up resigning from my job due to fact I couldn't do daily functions. I felt so guilty when it came to Joe. I was becoming incapable of the smallest things to the point it was a great day if I made it out of bed, to the couch and back into bed. All I did was cry. Joe was so precious, he asked what he could do and the answer was always "nothing". So he just sat next to me holding my hand or putting his arm around me.

One day I finally told him, this is not what he deserved. He needed someone he could live a good life with not with me. I gave him permission with my blessing to divorce me because I did not know what was wrong or if it would ever be alright again. I'd spent my whole life running from this black hole and this time it had swallowed me in its entirety. Joe refused to divorce me. I just wanted to die. Literally go to sleep and never wake up to another day. Joe was the only person I would answer the phone to. He would take me to the therapist due to driving being overwhelming for me. I could not even leave the house except for this therapist to see if he could help me. I couldn't go ahead and end my life because it would be Joe who would find me. I could not do that to him. The only person in my life I had ever been able to trust, love, feel secure and that genuinely cared about me.

The therapist said I was dealing with very deep depression and got together with my Dr. and put me on meds. I was so excited! To me, this would make me worthy of Joe again. Then they told me it would take four to six weeks to get into my system and begin working. The momentary cloud nine was gone in the blink of an eye. This was devastating to me. Joe was at every appointment, right beside me.

One day the therapist asked about my family. I laughed half-heartedly and said, "you must be joking". He continued to prod until I became angry and just laid it all out. The abuse by one, the neglect by the other, the brother that was all they cared about who was now a preacher and I had a baby brother who was probably the only one remotely close to normal, whatever that may be. Out of all I said, he said "so you're brother's a preacher? That means you have a good spiritual support. And since you brought up God, if's okay for me to talk to you about that". WHAT??? I let him know I did not have the same beliefs they did. If there was a GOD, then he wouldn't have let all this happen and no, I do not want to discuss my glorified preacher brother that's kept on a pedestal my whole life. I became very angry and was done. I had nothing more to say. Session over!

My days continued in this horrible black hole. I can remember actually making the bed one day and being so proud I had actually accomplished something. I was still sleeping or crying all the time. One day a green grasshopper got in the house and I would see him on the wall or the ceiling. I actually looked forward to finding the him each day. To me, it was like having a friend while not having to go anywhere. Hoppy (as we called him) was there every day.

As strange as the scenario sounds, I found a bit of solace in this silly little grasshopper.

There was a anti-depressant commercial that came out. It had this sad little egg that would go across the screen and it always made me burst out bawling. I mean ugly crying. I told Joe, "that's what's wrong with me. I don't have any happy eggs". More appointments, more of the meds, increase in the meds, tears, and sleep.

One morning Joe was off work and asked me to make him some breakfast. I thought he had lost his mind. I had not been able to accomplish anything other than making the bed in the last few weeks and he wanted me to cook? He just kept on about it. Finally, I was furious when I stood up and threw my blanket to the side, marched into the kitchen and literally threw open the refrigerator door, knocking stuff out onto the floor. Then I was really mad because I had to pick it all up. I grabbed for the eggs...that's when I saw them. Joe had drawn happy faces on all of them so I would have some happy eggs. I just melted to the floor and began sobbing. That was what he was wanting me to see. I did have some happy eggs after all! After he collected me off the floor, I attempted breakfast. I couldn't figure out what was wrong with the biscuits. It helps if you turn the oven on. This sent me into another spiral because I was so out of touch I couldn't even remember to turn the oven on!!!

I have no idea how Joe ever survived me.

One day sitting in the floor, utterly defeated, I just didn't want to have to wake up to another day EVER! I felt as though I was sitting at the gates of hell wishing I was inside. It had to be better than this. At that time, I cried out 'God help me'. I wasn't asking God to save me, I wanted the courage to take my own life. I cried out several times through uncontrollable sobs. I've never been fully able to explain what took place in my living room with me crumpled on the floor. Something changed. Something shifted. The tears stopped and I could feel another presence with me. He extended his hand to me and began lifting me out of all the darkness and despair. I could literally FEEL it falling away. I thought of my brother, how I'd never actually hated him but blamed him. None of it was his fault and he couldn't help that our parents had put such focus on him. The negative feelings I had toward him just fell away. You can say what you will but I know that I know, Jesus was in my living room with me and He was who was pulling me out of all this. The dramatic instant change is indescribable. I got up feeling whole, like I was in control of my own life and what I had been living was not it. I felt hope. The darkness was gone. The black hole didn't exist. I was full of joy, love and happiness. I couldn't wait for Joe to get home so I could tell him. I was so excited. Later I learned all those times he was sitting next to me holding my hand or with his arm around me, he was bargaining with God. He wanted God to prove to him that He was real and heal me. I wanted a bible. I needed to read about Jesus. Then Joe rededicated his life to Christ for now he believed.

I had told a friend my story and she gave me a Bible. I was ecstatic.....at first. I could not figure out what in the world it was saying. Nothing against the King James Version but I was having great difficulty.

Next I emailed my brother to find out the best bible for me to buy. He suggested the New American Standard Life Application Bible, so the next time we went to Oklahoma City, I bought it. I was not sure it was much better at first. I started reading in the New Testament and thought there was something wrong with it because the first three books were the same.

I continued reading, with many emails shot to my brother, with many questions. Then we talked about attending a church. He knew a Pastor that had moved to Enid and was the Senior Pastor of a church and encouraged me to go and at least try it. This was a church I'd heard a lot about during my time living in the Enid area and I didn't want to go there. I didn't want to be among rich snobby people and to my understanding, that is what this church was. However, I had wound up promising my brother I would try it. That Sunday, I drove into the parking lot and waited for the music to start. Going in, I sat near the back as not to be noticed. It was bad enough I was going to have to talk to this preacher and tell him who I was. But again, I had promised I would.

Nothing else will satisfy your soul cravings. Not marriage. Not a child. Not riches. Not things. Not a new car. Not a vacation. Not a dream house. Not a sport or hobby. Not sexual pleasure. Not food. Not alcohol. Not a sleeker body. Not plastic surgery. Not retirement. Not a getaway. Not anything. Only God. Only God alone.

-Author Unknown

The music was fantastic. I got totally lost in it, praising God. I noticed the young man in front of me raising his hands during worship and made a note to myself to check this out further afterwards. The sermon spoke directly to me, I was so glad I went!

When the sermon ended, I lingered. I had to wait and talk to this Pastor. The sanctuary was clearing out so I went and stood next to one of the sanctuary doors up against the paneling, still not wanting to be noticed. I was seriously fearful these people would never accept me. And then it happened. Where did she come from? This lady began talking to me and welcoming me. She told me a little about the church and things that were going on. The next thing I knew she had escorted me to the sign up center and I was signed up for a Bible Study, and to bring cookies back that evening. The cookies were for teachers at the school across the street the next morning. Her name was Tammy and I will never forget her. I was excited she was so nice and including me in things going on in the church! I had told Tammy that I was supposed to meet the Pastor so she took me right over to where he was. He seemed like a really nice, genuine guy. Very friendly. He introduced me to one of his sons. It was the young man that had been standing in front of me raising his hands.

When I left, I called my brother and told him all about it. I was so excited to go home, bake cookies and take them back with me to service that same night. When Joe got home from work, I told him all about it! When the evening service ended, he was as happy as I was about it. So began our spiritual journey at Enid First Assembly.

CHAPTER XII

KNOWLEDGE AND UNDERSTANDING

We rarely missed a service. Joe had to miss some Sunday mornings due to work but I took copious notes & would retell the sermon to him when he got home. One Sunday after church I just had to talk to the Pastor. I told Joe, he will either agree with me or kick us out, as we walked down the hall to his office. I told him what a great injustice I saw in people getting saved and then we just send them home. No warning of how difficult their new life may be or any direction at all! He was very sweet as he let us know he agreed and wanted to see us getting more involved. So, we started delivering welcome cookies to new guest's homes.

The medication I had been put on was working. I felt so good! So, I stopped taking it. Needless to say, I quit the meds twice and had to start taking them again. I hated having to have them. Then, a year later, I woke up one morning and went to take my meds and I knew God was telling me that I was done with them. I was able to stop taking them that day!! The meds had done wonders! I noticed little things I didn't see before. Individual leaves on trees and bushes, grasshoppers on the bush limbs, beautiful rose bushes, etc.

Then we began having prayer sessions. I

went to all of them. One day Pastor asked if we had plans for Tuesday evening. I told him we had to deliver cookies, and he said we could get someone else to do that and he wanted Joe and I to go to something in Oklahoma City the next Tuesday. It sounded as though a few others and some staff would go. We got there and it was only staff going. I felt so out of place, but we loaded up and went. There was speculation of where we were going, but no-one seemed to actually know. We all went to eat in Oklahoma City before continuing our journey. We arrived at another church and went in where worship was starting. They had a large service and then everyone broke down into small groups. There was a list of them and one was for women who had been abused. That's the one I chose. I was totally beside myself. Being in a room with other women and hearing them share about their experiences or the pain it had caused simply blew me away. There was a place to go and talk about these things while being given direction and classes you could sign up for? I was elated.

When we got back in the van to leave, everyone was asking Pastor about the trip and it's purpose. I made it known I couldn't wait for him to start this at our church. It was going to be life changing!!

Over the next couple of months I enquired about this new ministry and was told to pray about it. I did pray about it but did not see why we were not moving forward with it. There were people out there that needed it! Finally when asking about it yet again, the Pastor asked me if I had been praying about it. Naturally, I said yes and he said the strangest thing to me....okay, then listen! What? I thought I WAS listening and was supposed to be all in about this ministry and helping with it....which I was willing to be!

I went to his office once more...about the ministry. I left with full understanding I was being called to lead it. Why??? I hadn't been saved for very long, didn't know the first thing about ministry and how were we supposed to lead it? So, my husband and I visited churches in Oklahoma City and Tulsa to attend their ministry nights and visit with the people leading them to gain insight and learn how to do this correctly. I was as overwhelmed as I was excited. So was Joe! I worked the steps for the step study. I was so excited to get rid of even more baggage. However....I came to the part where we made an inventory list. A verse had caught my attention: Ephesians 4:31 (NIV) 31 Get rid of all bitterness, rage and anger, brawling and slander, along with every form of malice.

I was stunned. I knew that my inventory would need at LEAST a five subject spiral notebook to hopefully get it all written down!!! In this list I had to include myself in those who had wronged me and forgive God. It was then I realized I had blamed him for everything wrong in my life. But, I made it!

We got a group of Leaders together and took them through the steps so they knew exactly what to expect. We worked so hard on everything we would need for the ministry: name tags, shirts, information sheets, weekly service line-up, nursery workers, those to work sound and overhead projectors, etc. Joe and I had been in church a whopping year and a half as we launched Celebrate Recovery. I knew it would be hard because I know how resistant I had been when I didn't believe in God. We were willing and ready to put in the time and work to help others.

I want you to know the love that set me free. I don't worship a concept, I follow a KING.

-Author Unknown

Working the steps amazed me. I learned things about myself. Things I had no idea about. I learned (in addition to everything thus far) that I had had a relationship addiction, was co-dependent, alcohol was my way of escaping pain and most of all, I wasn't alone.

Working the steps was not all there was to a new life. I attended Bible Study, lead Bible Study and had my own personal time with God in my own studies at home. Every morning at 6am, I tuned in to The Potter's House! The studies, Potter's House and service made me who I am now as well as my marriage what it is. Some of the studies were hard. The more honest you are with yourself, the more you will get out of them. However, I finally understood the true meaning of Proverbs 9:10 The fear of the Lord is the beginning of wisdom, and knowledge of the Holy One is understanding.

Running Celebrate Recovery was a full time job, so, I ran it and volunteered at the church. Eventually I became a staff member, filling even more than I even knew I needed.

He's an "I don't care how far you've run, just come home" kind of God.

-Author Unknown

Joe and I could be so alike in some ways and so very different in others. Aren't we all? When something goes wrong, I simply meet it head on and take care of the problem developing the solution as I go. Joe on the other hand, assesses the situation, formulates a plan and then deploys it. This made me crazy at times. However, it turned out for the best. Sometimes he needs drawn out and sometimes I definitely needed reigned in.

Jessica blew out her knee and had to come home from the Army. It was devastating for her. She moved on and in a couple of years gave birth to our first grandson, Jayce. He had thick black hair and olive complexion. He was perfect.

It's extremely odd because I am truly one of the biggest extroverted introverts you will find. When I am out and about or working, I am all about getting it done. When I have been going full throttle, I will eventually wind up at home with what I refer to as a down day. It is simply a day where everything and everyone else can just wait. I need time for me to recharge. Sometimes I need it more than once a week. When I'm in downtime mode, people are not a part of my agenda. I don't want to be around anyone else, just Joe.

One of my Bible Studies taught me a huge amount about my marriage. What I say and what my husband hears are 2 different things. We're wired completely different. He's wired to be the provider, I'm wired to be the helpmate. It was almost outrageous because it was so true. One part talked about plumbing. This scenario had just happened at my home the previous week. A line was backing up and Joe was working to fix it. I simply said, 'just call the plumber and be done with it'. Now when I said that, I thought I was being helpful to my husband. He worked such long hours I didn't want him to have to spend his evening working on plumbing. But I learned the way he is wired, to him it was like I had said 'you aren't able to do that'. To him it was more of an insult and made him feel like he did not take care of me well enough. I am not talking about only my husband, I am talking about men in general. I'm simply telling you what I learned in Bible Study and it improved my marriage immensely.

The next week, the study talked about how men feel about a different scenario. If you say, we need new carpet this one is shot, or needs replaced, etc. He hears 'she doesn't think I provide well enough for her'. Again, in the last week I had said the words 'this carpet needs replaced, it's horrible'. It was a general statement, simply that, at some point, we need to replace. I never realized as the provider those words would cut him down.

I truly believe it fortified our marriage to learn these things. I became very aware of what and how I said things to him. Deep inside I wanted great communication with him. I wanted him to feel lifted up by me at all times. This was hard for me to keep in place at times when we had argued or I was mad at him. The truth is, those were times I needed to remember it even more so. So, I got in the practice of not only telling him but reminding myself of how wonderful he is. I made sure to tell him I loved him daily. At other times (not daily) I would be sure and let him know how much I appreciated him and all he did. Now remember...no one is always happy 24/7 so there were times I was saying it through clenched teeth. Not to him through clenched teeth, they were clenched while I was texting him. However, remember this - Strife cannot stay in the same place as gratitude. While you're being grateful, you cannot be mad at the same time. So, with this practice I started ending arguments or helped us reach a joint decision on solving problems. Be those problems kids, marriage, life, etc., we were making a difference in our lives, thoughts and most of all our marriage. God has lead us to, and shown us through, many things. Doing these things softened my heart and made me more conscientious of my thoughts and actions. No, that does not mean we have never had another disagreement or loud ones at that... it simply means I've learned how to handle it differently and make my marriage more fruitful. Something I had never had or known before. I learned I don't always have to be right. I've learned the value of my husband by praising him at all times.

Another study that was so much fun but we learned a tremendous amount about our differences was Laugh Your Way To A Better Marriage. And that is exactly what we did. It was so good we held a small group at our house and walked others through it as well.

All the time I sought for that 'key' to happiness…all along it was God's love. I had finally found the key to building a solid relationship. As long as I put God first, all else falls into place.

Chapter 12 - Knowledge And Understanding

CHAPTER XIII

GETTING REAL

Earlier, I mentioned my brother praying over us when we got married. Joe and I both fully know that the prayers set into motion on that day provided all the things we needed. His name was Jesus.

We had troubles and problems just like anyone else does. One night Joe was on his way home from work late at night and was pulled over. I had talked to him prior to this and was expecting him home any time. When he never showed up and didn't answer his phone, I went and drove the roads I believed he would have taken home. I spotted his jeep and was so elated!! I thought it had broken down or something. As I pulled up to the Jeep, I realized it was empty. An officer pulled up as I was looking in the jeep. I explained the situation and then he let me know when the officer ran Joe's information, he was arrested - saying he had a warrant for a DUI. It was too late to try to do anything. I went and got Jessica so we could get the Jeep home before it was impounded. I called the attorney the next morning but Joe had already been released. It had been a false arrest of the wrong person due to information being entered incorrectly. It was such a crazy night and I was so glad to have him back home.

Remember Mark from the first section of this story? He tried to make life hell. One of the stipulations in our joint custody was for me to show him my rent and utilities receipts. After doing that for several months, I showed up with them one day for him to see. He shook his head and said you don't have to keep bringing these. They're basically always the same. Remember, he said we would keep joint custody with no child support if I gave him the whole sale of our house? Yeah, he took me to court for child support. In court, he actually claimed I had never followed the stipulation of showing him my receipts so he had no idea what my rent or bills were. This was used against me and I didn't stand a chance since it was he said, she said about the house, the stipulation for receipts, etc. Don't take me wrong, I wanted the kids taken care of which had worked out great until he remarried. Then he suddenly didn't remember any of the things he had said. This was drawn out over several years. Eventually, our son came to live with us and our daughter lived with him in the end. I say this just to help show, everything wasn't just peaches and cream. We still walked through some horrendous situations. BUT, we walked through them gracefully and with that peace that passes all understanding.

We were blessed with a beautiful granddaughter, Grace. She had blonde hair and brown eyes and was so very tiny. Just as Grace was turning 1 year old, we found out she had a very rare genetic disease called Canavan's. They told us all the things she would never do and concluded with our needing to make her funeral arrangements. We refused to accept that as the final say. Over her first three years, she did many things the Dr.'s had said she would never do. Don't take me wrong, there were special needs and it was difficult on Jessica. However, Jessica was determined to do all she could to help Grace thrive.

Joe and I have had a blessed life. I don't want you to think we don't but we have the same problems everyone else had, we simply learned to handle them differently.

We take vacations like anyone else but our vacations are few and far between. When we do get to go, we enjoy every moment of it and we both know God has blessed us beyond measure. We love to go to Jamaica. It's beauty is breathtaking. The countryside is amazing, especially when you get off the tourist path. I say all of this simply to tell you, we've been able to do things and go places neither of us had ever dreamed of. But first, we had to get our hearts in order and be available to the ways God has used us. Our children are blessed. Jessica is happily married and gave birth to our youngest grandson, Jett. Victoria is thriving with her family. She also gave us a granddaughter, Brianna. Dillon went on and became an electrician in the oil field. Shelby got her BSN and gave us another beautiful granddaughter, Sawyer. The back of her hair is very curly just like Shelby's was when she was little. We're very proud of the lives our children live.

We've suffered many things just as anyone does. The death of Joe's mother, Rose. Everyone loved Rose. She was so lighthearted and had the best sense of humor. She used to tell me that she wished Joe had met me when he was much younger. I had to agree. I was always, and still am, thankful to her for her son and how she raised him. The wonderful man he turned out to be. They had a rough life but in the end were living great lives.

Ten months later we suffered the death of our granddaughter, two weeks prior to her turning four. It was a horrible phone call from my daughter. The ambulance was there to take

Grace to the ER. Jessica couldn't go at that time due to DHS coming out and the city cops were there. I got to the hospital before Jessica did. I can never describe the horrible sinking feeling when the Dr. came out and asked if the mother was there yet. I explained what was going on and he had authorities release her to get down there. He then shared that Grace had passed. They let me go back to be with her. It was absolutely horrible to hold her little hand and hug her. She was soo cold. She looked like she was sleeping but was a blue/grey shade. Gut wrenching to say the least. When Jessica arrived the chaplain was unaware she didn't know yet and went up, introduced himself and let her know he was there if she needed anything, he was there for her. Instantly she knew Grace had died. As if all of this weren't about more than I could handle, Jessica and I went back to see Grace. Of course, Jessica totally lost it, picked up Grace and collapsed to the floor in a wale of tears flowing. Once we finally left that area, there were welfare workers waiting for her in the waiting room. I was beside myself. They were asked to leave and I was so thankful. The welfare services made sure our five year old grandson thought his sisters' death was his fault. They did not care what kind of damage they did by putting those thoughts in his head, they just wanted someone to blame. It took a lot to convince our precious grandson that no one blamed him. Those people just had to ask him stupid questions to make sure they felt like they had done their job. The spiral it threw our daughter into was unimaginable. Jayce stayed with us. That first night I was rocking him and asked if he wanted to lay on the couch and watch tv. He turned to me and put a precious little hand on each of my cheeks and said "GiGi, you don't want to go to sleep by me or you might get dead". I was beyond heartbroken at these words. I told him that would definitely not happen. So we laid on the couch until we fell asleep. The next day we had to go to the funeral home to make arrangements. It was all so surreal. How could we be sitting here, doing this and she wasn't even quite four yet?

A few years later, we dealt with the death of my grandfather. My grandfather - all I could think was at least one person had stood with me against the sexual abuse. That had increased our relationship tremendously.

In one year, Joe and I both wound up have emergency surgeries. Joe had gone in for a stress test. His mother had heart disease and based on some things Joe was telling the cardiologist, it was decided to do a heart catheter on him. It turned out the main artery into his heart was ninety-five percent clogged. He was admitted and surgery was performed the next morning. It was one of the most grueling things I've been through. When he first came out of surgery, I couldn't hold his hand or talk to him for several hours. God gave me the strength to walk through this gracefully yet the grace to fall apart when I was alone and either just cry in His presence with no words needed or simply talk to Him through or after the tears. I had great difficulty trying to take care of Joe due to only being six months post op myself. I had a five pound football shaped tumor removed that had done damage and required a total hysterectomy as well. Due to the size of the tumor, it couldn't be done laparoscopically. I had to do the old fashioned surgery. But together, we made it. Joe was there every step of the way during my recovery. It took three months for me just to get back to work and that was only part-time. So, I don't want you to think we have this fabulous glory life without strife or pain. We do. We just handle it all much differently than what I had known previously.

I finally understood

We ran Celebrate Recovery with all of our heart. Women and men recovering from a multitude of things were more important to us than anything else. I learned the majority of women's addictions stemmed from sexual abuse as a child. I didn't want them to have to suffer any longer. Their freedom was of utmost importance to me.

Freedom for those who suffer from abuse is my heartbeat. My heart breaks every single day for broken women everywhere. I'm amazed at how many women will share their stories with me. They're all over the world. If you don't know a sexually abused woman or man...they don't trust you. This is a sacred secret to the one who experienced it. I am beyond blessed by the many women who have shared through their sobs and pain.

You don't have to suffer alone. I want each and every hurting soul to get the help they need and allow God to set them free from those demons. Those demons come in many different forms: No/Low self-esteem, self harm, eating disorders, sexual addiction, co-dependency, spending addictions and the list goes on and on.

I allowed four people to read the very beginning pages of this book as I started writing it. I'm still amazed. All 4 wound up sharing about the abuse they suffered years ago and how it still affects them today. One of them had never told anyone…she is married and has grandchildren and had suffered all these years alone. Another had only ever told one person and it wasn't their spouse. Again, married with children and grandchildren. Another who had recently moved to another state and didn't tell her family, shared with me about her abuse,

If you're balking about God right now, remember….I would have also at one time.

Forgiveness - it's not condoning what happened to you. It is not truly even for them. It is for YOU. It is so you can live a happy, fulfilling life.

We no longer run a Celebrate Recovery. I know that God told me to step away from it so He could remove the stigma because there were women everywhere that needed to hear what I had and they wouldn't dare go to Celebrate Recovery. I know everyone thinks it's only for drugs and alcohol. It is not. It is for SO MUCH MORE.

I know God wants to see your healing. To see you happy. So do I. So does your family. My beliefs don't have to be yours. You can worship who/whatever you want. All I want is to see/know you've been set free.

If you're struggling, I want to offer you a group you can join. In this group, you are not alone. You'll hear about other women who experienced the same things you have. Stories of hope and happiness. It is a Facebook Group - Abused & Beautifully Redeemed: https://www.facebook.com/groups/585261405323807/

You NEED to know you are loved, lovable and you are not hopeless, helpless or the many other negative thoughts you have. Please feel free to send a personal message if you're not ready to be in the discussion yet.

As hard as it has been to write about all my faults, negativities and screw ups.....it is all worth it if one life is changed. I don't think I truthfully realized just how messed up I really was until I wrote all this down. The craziest part is those are just the highlight reels. If you think I sound crazy...well, you're probably correct.

Back then I was definitely not right.

So I thank you for allowing me to share my chaos with you. It has deepened my love for God who saved & redeemed me.

You survived what you thought would kill you. Now straighten your crown and move forward like the queen you are.

-Author Unknown

Meet
LAURA
SCHONLAU

Born in Oklahoma, Laura has a huge heart for broken/hurting women. Being abused as a child gives her an ability to relate to them by hearing more than just their words. She hears their hearts and the underlying hurt. She has endured all of the emotions they go through; pain, hate, low self-esteem, unforgiveness, and the tears. The many, many tears she has shed, just like them, and for them. She has spent the last eighteen years helping women help themselves, move to places of forgiveness, and build self-esteem.

This book was published by

FIRST TIME
PRESS

10% of all the revenue from this book goes
to support missions work. We hope you enjoyed
this author's self-edited work.

First Time Press exists to give promising authors a platform to publish their early works. Since its founding, First Time Press has eagerly sought out and received submissions from authors worldwide looking for a chance to be noticed for their extraordinary work.

Each year, First Time Press receives self-submitted manuscripts from undiscovered authors looking to use their talents to bring God glory. Each work is reviewed and examined by an award-winning team of creators. Five manuscripts are hand-picked each year for their raw excellence (ranging anywhere from sci-fi to biographies). These manuscripts are then edited by the author and published "as is" to showcase the creator's undiscovered talent.

First Time Press looks to encourage and celebrate the achievements of those who have a passion and a calling to write. All publishing expenses are covered, and there is no out of pocket cost for these authors once chosen for publication. 80% of all revenue generated from the sales of First Time Press books is given back to their respective authors. Only 20% is deducted, 10% to cover the cost of operations and 10% donated to missions.

Other titles from

FIRST TIME
PRESS

Other Worlds and their stories
By J. Riley Peak

The question regarding whether or not other planets share earth's unique ability to rear life is a question many ask. However, I resign myself to the idea that I must leave such a search alone, for why bother talking about planets when one can speak about worlds?

Hearts at War
By Rob Winblad

Sergeant Rick Newman has shipped to Afghanistan with the Marines. After a mission goes wrong and his fiancee's brother is killed in action, he blames himself for her brother's death. Running from the demons that haunt him, he must find it in his heart to forgive himself, even as she has forgiven him.

The Torch Keepers
By Hosanna Emily

A revolution sweeps across the kingdom of Érkeos. A girl finds her city engulfed in the Liberation's emerald flames. But, when she meets Rekém, she rebels against the King. Now Kadira and Rekém could bring destruction to the entire kingdom.